Problems and Possibilities for Religious Education

Studies in Teaching and Learning
General Editor
Denis Lawton, B.A., Ph.D.
Professor of Education and Deputy Director,
University of London Institute of Education

In the series:

Denis Lawton *An Introduction to Teaching and Learning*
John Robertson *Effective Classroom Control*
Maurice Holt *Evaluating the Evaluators*
Richard Aldrich *An Introduction to the History of Education*
Edwin Cox *Problems and Possibilities for Religious Education*
Denis Lawton *Curriculum Studies and Educational Planning*
Richard Pring *Personal and Social Development*
Frieda Painter *Schooling for the Gifted*
Patrick D. Walsh *Values in Teaching and Learning*
Maggie Ing *Psychology, Teaching and Learning*

Problems and Possibilities for Religious Education

Edwin Cox

HODDER AND STOUGHTON

LONDON SYDNEY AUCKLAND TORONTO

British Library Cataloguing in Publication Data

Cox, Edwin
  Problems and possibilities for religious education.
  —(Studies in teaching and learning)
  1. Religious education—Great Britain
  I. Title   II. Series
  200'.7'1041   BL42.5.G7

  ISBN 0 340 28433 1

First published 1983

Printed and bound in Great Britain for
Hodder and Stoughton Educational,
a division of Hodder and Stoughton Ltd,
Mill Road, Dunton Green, Sevenoaks, Kent,
by Richard Clay (The Chaucer Press) Ltd, Bungay, Suffolk.

Typeset in 11 on 12pt Plantin (Linotron) by
Rowland Phototypesetting Ltd.

Contents

Studies in Teaching and Learning

The purpose of this series of short books on education is to make available readable, up-to-date views on educational issues and controversies. Its aim will be to provide teachers and students (and perhaps parents and governors) with a series of books which will introduce those educational topics which any intelligent and professional educationist ought to be familiar with. One of the criticisms levelled against 'teacher-education' is that there is so little agreement about what ground should be covered in courses at various levels; one assumption behind this series of texts is that there is a common core of knowledge and skills that all teachers need to be aware of, and the series is designed to map out this territory.

Although the major intention of the series is to provide general coverage, each volume will consist of more than a review of the relevant literature; the individual authors will be encouraged to give their own personal interpretation of the field and the way it is developing.

Preface

Seventeen years ago I wrote a book called *Changing Aims in Religious Education* which some have been kind enough to say has had a small influence on the development of religious education since that time. A casual glance at this book may suggest that it is a grown up Son of Changing Aims; but that would be a mistake. This is, in many respects, a more personal book. Dealing with religious education over a space of more than thirty years leads one to certain views about it, and I have tried to set them out here as a contribution to the continuing debate about the place of the study of religion in the school curriculum. They are put forward in the hope that they may be helpful, rather than in the confidence that they solve all the problems. If the dogmatism that comes with age has led me to express views with an unwarranted assurance, or to argue for them insufficiently, I ask the reader's forgiveness.

In particular, apologies are offered to half of the human race for having always referred to the teacher as 'he'. I recognise freely that this is male, chauvinist, piggish and inaccurate. But since English has no third person singular neuter pronoun that can properly be applied to persons, and I am not yet acclimatised to using the novel s/he, choice had to be made of a gender to avoid the tiresome repetition of 'he or she'. Fortunately or unfortunately, I was born male and, fortunately or unfortunately, most of my school teaching experience has been in establishments which were predominantly masculine, and consequently it comes more easily to me to refer to a teacher as 'he'. I have therefore used this form in the confident hope that my female colleagues will redress the balance in their books by always writing of the teacher as 'she'.

A word of explanation may be needed of the way in which I have, in this writing, used the word 'religion'. I have applied the term to the human search for meaning and value in experience when that search is conducted in the context of a theistic belief, and when the search is set against a non-theistic background I have used the phrase 'life-stance'. It will be pointed out that this usage is, in a way, idiosyncratic, and that to many who practise a religion it does not appear to be anything like that, being rather a pattern of life and formal observance which they have accepted naturally as part of their received culture, or which has been divinely revealed to them, without any searching on their part. Nevertheless, that received pattern ought to have the effect of giving shape and purpose to their lives (even if they are not continually conscious that it is doing so). At its best, religion ought to include striving for greater clarity of insight into reality and re-search into keener perception of the significance and purpose of experience. If it has lost that motivation and been reduced to an unexamined acceptance of a life pattern that may explain why it has lost so much of its significance for many of our contemporaries. It also raises the question of whether religion so conceived is of sufficient import to be worth studying in schools.

Gratitude is due to the many teachers, and to my students over the years, who have agreed, disagreed, and argued with me about the meaning of religion and the purpose of religious education and thereby helped fashion the ideas I have used in this writing. Some will be able to recognise their contribution more readily than others, but all have had their influence. The book is dedicated to them, in the hope that they will find it sensible enough for that dedication to be a compliment.

London, 1983   Edwin Cox

The Past

1 The Religious Provisions and the Intentions of the 1944 Education Act

The first schools in Great Britain were provided by religious agencies, and it was assumed that religion would be taught in them. The Board Schools that followed Forster's 1870 Education Act generally included a religious element in their curriculum. Between 1870 and the First World War bitter controversy often raged about the nature of the religious instruction that was permissible, but it concerned denominational differences rather than dispute about the desirability of including in the syllabus the teaching of what were widely accepted religious tenets.

Prior to 1944 religious education was visualised as teaching children to be Christian, and since Christianity was equated with its fairly rigid doctrinal forms, this meant attaching pupils to a particular denomination. Denominations with well-established schools tended to see this as a method of recruiting adherents, while the others thought it gave their rivals an unfair advantage. The matter was complicated by the existence of areas where the only school was a denominational one, and those who belonged to other churches feared that their children were likely to be indoctrinated with unacceptable ideas. Yet behind the controversy was a deep conviction that some religious teaching was necessary for the psychological well-being of the pupils and for their moral training. Consequently, when narrow denominational considerations were transcended, even the fiercest controversialists agreed that at least a knowledge of the Bible would do no one any harm and might even do some students an amount of good. Thus study of the Bible 'without note or comment'[1] was the minimum to be found in all schools, whereas in a good number much more was taught besides.

By 1944, as a result of the ecumenical movement, denominational rivalry had considerably subsided. Christian denominations were less bitterly opposed and suspicious of each other, and it was felt that there was sufficient common ground for them to be able to agree on a programme of religious teaching in schools. The way had already been shown by the production of 'Agreed Syllabuses' in certain areas, Cambridge, for instance, having produced one as early as 1924. In this eirenic spirit the 1944 Act made teaching of religion a legal requirement in all schools.

The legislators seem to have envisaged more than the imparting of information. They stipulated that there should also be religious observance, and that is mentioned in the Act before instruction.

The school day in every county school and in every voluntary school shall begin with collective worship on the part of all pupils in attendance at the school, and arrangements made therefore shall provide for a single act of worship attended by all such pupils.[2]

Religious instruction shall be given in every county school and in every voluntary school.[3]

It has been customary for later commentators to attack the use of the term 'religious instruction' in the Act, on the grounds that this shows an over-authoritarian view of education, and in recent years the term 'religious education' has been preferred. This is not entirely just, for the shoulder notes of the relevant section of the Act use the term 'religious education' to cover the two elements of worship and classroom teaching of religion viewed as a whole. When, therefore, the draftsman came to the clause dealing with the classroom teaching, he had to find another name, and since he had used 'secular instruction' in the headings of the preceding group of sections, 'religious instruction' probably seemed appropriate here. The subject may have been viewed in a less doctrinaire and illiberal light than is sometimes supposed.

Nevertheless, there were in the Act escape clauses[4] which allowed parents to withdraw their children if they did not wish them to learn religion or to take part in a form of worship, and this suggests that there was an underlying intention that the subject should make pupils religious in some way. These clauses imply that the teaching was different from what it was in other subjects. It was attempting something to which there could be conscientious objection in a way that there could not be to mathematics or music.

Though the wording of the Act never specifies what religion was to be taught, and what type of worship was to be conducted, it was assumed that Christianity was intended, and probably Protestant Christianity in particular. There were possibly a number of reasons for this. The word 'religion', rather than 'Christianity', may have been chosen out of deference to a minority of Jewish schools and Jewish pupils. It could be that Parliament felt that, much as it might wish for social and moral purposes that the 'religious consciousness . . . latent in every boy and girl and in every man and woman should be awakened and strengthened',[5] it ought not to lend its overt approval to any specific form of organised religion, much less to the formularies or catechisms of any denomination. More likely, the insular British outlook of the time, having less contact with world faiths than we have now, assumed that Christianity was the only form of religion that was respectable enough to be studied and practised. That when the Bill said 'religion' the word 'Christianity' was to be read is clearly shown in many of the speeches made in support of it in both Houses.

> . . . it is the intention of the Government and of the Bill that the religious instruction required to be given shall be Christian instruction, and that the corporate act of worship shall be an act of Christian worship.[6]

That this was the intention is further borne out by the type of Agreed Syllabuses produced immediately after the passing of the Act. Having legislated for religious education, Parliament handed over the definition of it to the representatives of the Churches and the educational administrators by requiring that the teaching in all maintained schools should be according to an Agreed Syllabus, and that such syllabuses should be largely used in church schools that were designated 'controlled', and in those that were classed as 'aided' when parents requested it. Each local authority had to draw up its own syllabus or adopt one made by another authority. These syllabuses had (and still have) to be approved by a Syllabus Conference consisting of four panels, one representing the Church of England, one representing 'other religious denominations', one representing the local education authority and one representing teachers' organisations. The panels have equal status and for a topic to be included in the syllabus it must be approved by all four, which, in effect, gives each a right of veto. In the early days no religion other than Christianity was included on the conferences and the theological and ecclesiastical representatives seem to have had a decisive influence, with the result that the syllabuses produced between 1944 and 1960 are schemes of Christian study, being largely Biblical in content, but including a certain amount of Church history and Christian doctrine. The Surrey syllabus (1947) went a little further and introduced for senior pupils a section on 'Problems of Religion and Life', but even that stated in its preamble that its general aim was to give children 'knowledge of the common Christian faith held by their fathers for 2,000 years' and to help them 'seek for themselves in Christianity principles which give purpose to life and a guide to all its problems' (p.6). Similarly, the Birmingham syllabus of the same year stated that 'Pupils should be made to realise that no other standards . . . can give so satisfactory and complete a solution to their problems as those based on the mission and message of Jesus' (p.5), and the Sunderland Borough Syllabus (1944) saw the goal of religious teaching as 'a life of worship and service in the Christian community' (p.13). These statements are typical of the syllabuses of the time, which show, both in their contents and in their statements of intent, that the religious instruction that the 1944 Act enjoined was intended to be instruction in, and possibly conversion to, Christianity.

It may be worth noting in passing that these syllabuses assumed that all children come from homes that are sympathetic to Christianity and are anxious to learn of the Christian faith and practice; that there is a body of agreed theological truth which can be transmitted in classroom teaching; that knowledge of the Bible will have some beneficial influence on character and produce in its students a religious faith; and that children of all ages think about religion in the same way and are equally capable of, and in need of, religious faith. In discussions about religious education in the past two and a half decades all these assumptions have been called in question.

Looking back from our present age of scepticism and religious pluralism, it is difficult to understand why the nation in 1944 committed itself to such a thorough-going programme of Christian teaching.[7] One extreme explanation is that it was a conscious attempt on the part of the nation to Christianise itself. This was expressed by Spencer Leeson in 1947, when he wrote, 'Parliament has declared the will of the nation that it shall be a Christian nation; and the state-aided schools are to do their part by teaching the nation's children to worship and understand.'[8] Thirty years later, Edward Norman put forward a similar view:

The Act has come to be understood by the advocates of change as an attempt by a Christian society of the past to safeguard beliefs which are no longer widely subscribed. That is a misunderstanding. It was not how those who enacted the legislation saw it at all – as reference to *Hansard* will verify. The religious provisions were intended as an initiative to Christianise society, to make people *more* aware of Christianity, not merely to hold the line.[9]

At the other extreme, attempts have been made to explain the religious provisions of 1944 as a case of horse-trading between the Government and the Churches to facilitate the transfer of schools to the control of the local education authority.[10] The Churches had a greater say in education then than they have now, because they owned so many of the schools. The Act stipulated far higher standards of accommodation and more spacious school buildings. The Church schools tended to be old and in need of more modernisation than their owners could afford in order to bring them up to the required standards. At the same time, those aging buildings were necessary to the educational system and the State could not allow the schools they housed to cease to function. Consequently, the State offered to take over any ecclesiastical schools whose owners were prepared to relinquish them rather than face the expense of modernisation. Apart from the Roman Catholics, no Church made obviously strenuous efforts to retain all its schools and many voluntary schools passed into 'controlled' status in the years following the 1944 Act. It is possible that the religious provisions of the Bill influenced and facilitated this process. The Churches' influence and property stake in education would enable them to bargain for the presence of religious teaching in schools, and they may have been more ready to accept voluntary controlled status for their schools when they had been assured that this teaching would continue in them.

The former of these extreme views may be too sanguine, the latter too cynical. A deeper but more diffuse influence was a desire to protect the values underlying liberal democracy. This was comparatively new (complete universal suffrage had been achieved in Great Britain only in 1928) and depended on an active concern for, and pursuit of, moral values by citizens. Traditionally those values had been linked to religious beliefs, and there was a widespread, diffuse and often muddle-headed assumption that this was still the case. The rise of a different set of values in Fascist countries constituted a direct challenge to liberal democracy, and Britain had embarked reluctantly on the Second World War to meet that challenge. In the early years of the war, there was a spirit of crusade, and a *Times* leader was able to describe the war as a fight for Christian principles.

> Each month of the war shows its real nature more clearly. The issue lies between the fundamental precepts of Christianity, shared as they are by millions in other lands and of other religions, and a force which is consciously and resolutely vowed to their destruction.[11]

It seemed illogical to spend the whole of the nation's effort, and demand the death of thousands of the nation's citizens, if at the end of it the standards for which the country had fought were not maintained in its own life and teaching. To quote *The Times* again:

> The truth is . . . that education with religion omitted is not really education at all . . . It will be of little use to fight, as we are fighting today, for the preservation of Christian principles if Christianity itself is to have no future, or at immense cost to safeguard religion against attack from without if we allow it to be starved by neglect from within . . .
>
> Christianity cannot be imbibed from the air. It is not a philosophy but a historic religion which must dwindle unless the facts on which it is founded are taught, and such teaching made the centre of our educational system.[12]

The concern for religious and traditional values is considered to be the fundamental purpose of religious education by the White Paper, *Educational Reconstruction*.

> There has been a very general wish not confined to representatives of the Churches, that religious education should be given a more definite place in the life and work of the schools, springing from the desire to revive the spiritual and personal values in our society and in our national tradition.[13]

That statement suggests that religious education was envisaged by its writers not as merely giving information about religions, or as promoting any particular religious interest, but as something deeper, as inculcating certain values on which the life of the nation, as then organised, depended. This view found champions in R. A. Butler and William Temple. The one a politician, the other an ecclesiastic, these men had a similar social and educational background, and looked at the State from a common point of view. Butler was a churchwarden, and Temple a headmaster before he became an archbishop. The latter, during his brief tenure of the Archbishopric of Canterbury, won a considerable prestige in all sections of the community. He saw the State as founded on moral principles which are ultimately religious, and his book *Christianity and the Social Order*[14] attempted to show how those principles should apply in practice. For him it was the responsibility of the Church (and by 'Church' he meant all Christian citizens and not merely the established Church of England) to bear witness to those principles, to subject them to constant scrutiny, and continually to draw them to the attention of the country's legislators without being identified with any particular party. Church and State were partners in upholding democratic values, the Church proclaiming, purifying them, and providing their rationale by its doctrines, the State arranging for them to be expressed in practice. Religious education was one example of this collaboration, and Temple's wish to see it properly conducted in all the nation's schools sprang from a desire to further the welfare of all the citizens of the democratic state, and not merely to propagate a creed held by only some of them. His prestige and statesmanship facilitated the passing of the religious clauses of the Act.

The view held by Temple and Butler of the relationship of community values and religion was echoed, in a diffuse way, in the minds of most people of the time. That is not to say that the general public were avidly demanding religious education. Many were probably unaware, as they usually are, of what was being enacted, in their name, by Parliament. Furthermore the Act dealt with matters other than religion. It extended secondary education to all suitable to 'their differing ages, abilities and aptitudes'.[15] It envisaged greatly improved and increased standards of accommodation. These were major advances in the educational system, compared with which the religious clauses may have seemed insignificant to a nation preoccupied with the wartime struggle for survival. Those religious clauses, though they were closely argued in the preliminary negotiations between the Churches and in Parliament, did not arouse keen public concern, and may have been accepted by a large portion of the nation as part of a package deal, because the other ingredients of the package seemed worth having. Even so, if pressed, all except extreme secularists would have agreed with Temple that ultimately the traditional values of the country had their basis in a religious view of life and that such a view should be propagated in the interest of democratic freedom and good order. Most would probably have expressed that feeling in a more pragmatic way. They would have related religious education with helping the young to be good. Under the general dislocation of the times, when many parents were parted from their families, and those remaining at home were working long hours, and when children in danger areas were evacuated to live with strangers, the standards of juvenile behaviour were beginning to deteriorate. Juvenile delinquency was not yet a major problem, but it was starting to be noticed. This may have led parents to ask for religious education as a means of combating this unwelcome manifestation, of re-establishing traditional standards and of promoting moral education and moral motivation.

What, in retrospect, seems strange about this national commitment to nationwide religious education is that those who welcomed it for their children were not, on the whole, closely attached to religious organisations or particularly anxious to show their beliefs by indulging in religious practices and attending regularly at public worship. Church-going was declining and most people, although content to pay lip-service to the ideals of religion, were inclined to be cautious of admitting to specific religious obligations. The church-going minority might hold a theological, ecclesiastical, sacramental religion which included precise beliefs and duties, but to the others religion was something more diffuse. They had a 'folk religion'[16] rather than an ecclesiastical one, the sort of undefined religion that Kenneth Hyde called a 'subterranean theology'.

> These beliefs are thematic in form, not systematically elaborated, and bear little reference to the beliefs and practices of the recognised religious denominations. Christianity is seen primarily as a system of ethics – doing good, helping lame dogs, and living decently. Prayer or religious belief is seen to have an efficacy that pre-supposes some kind of supernatural power; such belief is thought to be natural, most people were brought up to believe in this way.[17]

Probably the greater part of the legislators who voted for the Act had something similar in mind. But they did not see it as their responsibility to state precisely how the religious education they required should be conducted. For one thing, they were politicians and not educationists; for another, although they supported religion in general, they were not prepared to support any particular form of it. Sir Harold Webbe, in the debate on the White Paper, said:

> . . . the State cannot – and I would say, should not, take upon itself the full responsibility for fostering the distinctive formulas of particular denominations.[18]

Consequently, the responsibility of defining religious education was handed over to the local authorities and the 'experts', who were, by their Agreed Syllabuses, to find some measure of agreement between religious bodies and define what was to be taught. As we have seen, the Agreed Syllabus Conferences contained a high proportion of churchmen and theological scholars, whose influence was decisive.[19] They were not concerned with a folk faith, but with something more ecclesiastical, and their theology tended to be specific rather than 'subterranean'. The syllabuses they produced were probably too church-orientated and too doctrinally expressed to suit the taste of a folk faith. They spoke to the church-going minority (whose assumptions they shared) rather than to the generality of parents and pupils. Which is perhaps why the religious teaching that followed the 1944 Education Act failed to achieve the success that was hoped. It presupposed an attitude in the community which had been largely abandoned, and which was to be further modified drastically in the next three decades.

NOTES

1 This was the formula suggested by T. H. Huxley for use in the London Board Schools to prevent denominational interpretations being placed upon scripture during its study in schools.

2 1944 Education Act, Sect. 25.1.

3 Ibid., Sect. 25. 2.

4 Ibid., Sect. 25. 4.

5 From a speech by Sir Harold Webbe in the debate on the White Paper *Educational Reconstruction* (1943). Parliamentary Debates (Hansard) 5th Series, H. C. 391, 1856–9.

6 Parliamentary Debates (Hansard) 4th Series, 132, 366.

7 For a thorough-going analysis of the social and political pressures that contributed to the framing of the religious clauses of the 1944 Act, see Dennis Starkings' unpublished M.A. thesis (Starkings, 1980). (Bibliographical references will be found between pages 145–8.)

8   Spencer Leeson, *Christian Education* (Leeson, 1947, p. 194).

9   E. R. Norman, 'The Threat to Religion' (Norman, 1977, p. 103).

10   The term 'horse-trading' was applied to the settlement by Christopher Price, M.P., in a television discussion, in which the writer took part, in 1974. It may be too harsh. But there is a hint of political compromise in R. A. Butler's autobiographical *The Art of the Possible* (Butler, 1971, p. 99), where he writes: 'An important development which met the wishes of the Nonconformists and of many Anglicans was the "agreed syllabus". Because of this many Anglican managers were willing to hand over their schools to the local authorities in return for Christian teaching on these lines.'

11   *The Times*, 13 February 1941.

12   *The Times*, 17 February 1940.

13   Board of Education, *Educational Reconstruction*, H.M.S.O., 1943, p. 36.

14   Published by Penguin Books, 1942.

15   The phrase used in the Act (Sect. 8, 1.) to justify the tripartite system, of Grammar, Technical and Secondary Modern schools.

16   The expression is used by D. N. Hardy in 'Teaching religion: a theological critique', in *Learning for Living*, 15, 1, Autumn 1975.

17   K. E. Hyde, 'The home, the community and the peer group' (Hyde, 1975).

18   Parliamentary Debates (Hansard) 5th Series, H.C. 391, 1856–9.

19   The conference that produced the Cambridgeshire Syllabus of 1949 included eleven academics (among them C. H. Dodd, R. H. Thouless, C. F. D. Moule and W. O. Chadwick), three theological college principals, two training college principals, a Diocesan Director of Education, ten head teachers (two of them from public schools with a religious foundation) and six other teachers, one of whom was a school chaplain.

2 Influences for Change Since 1944

After a dozen years of statutory Agreed Syllabus religious education it was natural that interested parties should begin to enquire
how far it was succeeding. Perhaps it was too early to expect any
startling results, but there had been no obvious increase in
national godliness. On the contrary, church-going had further
declined and juvenile delinquency had increased. Nor had the
subject aroused noteworthy enthusiasm in the majority of pupils,
or gained the admiration of teachers of other disciplines. Some
sort of assessment seemed needed.

The first investigation was that commissioned by the Institute
of Christian Education and conducted by Dr Basil Yeaxlee in
conjunction with Birmingham University. Dr Yeaxlee's report,
produced in 1957 and entitled *Religious Education in Schools*,[1]
showed that the teaching was meeting at best with mixed success,
but because it was a personal impression, based on interviews with
teachers and containing no statistics, its cautiously written conclu-
sions caused little comment.

In 1961 appeared two books about the religious learning of
pupils in secondary modern schools which sparked off a discussion of the nature of the subject which has been going on ever
since. These were a report produced by Sheffield University
Institute of Education entitled *Religious Education in Secondary
Schools*[2] and Harold Loukes's *Teenage Religion*.[3] The former
showed that many children were not retaining more than a little of
what they were being taught, and the latter pointed out that they
were misunderstanding most of what they were remembering.
Teenage Religion, which was an impressionistic rather than a
statistical survey, was written in an engaging style, quoted at
length from what the pupils had written, including their infelici-
ties of expression and eccentric spellings; it was widely read and

proved something of a catalyst. The significant conclusion of this book was that pupils at the top of the secondary modern school had a live interest in religion and a sensitivity to religious issues, but that the teaching they were receiving did not seem to them to relate to that interest. What was being placed before them appeared a collection of meaningless statements, which they recalled in a confused and distorted fashion. Pupils had religious feeling, but no religious language in which to express it, and so showed 'little sign of a constructive framework of thought and intelligible belief'.[4]

Attention having been thus drawn to the fact that religious education, though not failing entirely, was far from being wholly successful, the next step was to enquire why so much devoted effort on the part of teachers of the subject was producing so little result. Practical difficulties, such as small time-table allocation, lack of equipment, unsympathetic head teachers and scarcity of trained specialists, were only half answers, and looked like excuses, for had the teaching proved an obvious educational success these disabilities would have been removed. The first place where an explanation was sought was in the psychology of religious development in children. Perhaps they didn't all think about religion in precisely the same way at all ages so that the teaching was not suited to their needs at certain stages of growth. Investigation into this had already been started by R. J. Goldman and K. E. Hyde, working independently and in slightly different fields at Birmingham University, and their findings, coming at an apposite time, evoked great interest.

Goldman was concerned with investigating how far the development of religious thinking in children followed the pattern described by Piaget for the development of thinking in general, proceeding from the pre-operational, through the concrete, to the abstract.[5] The research was wide-ranging, complex and sophisticatedly statistical and its findings were published with great panache, with the result that for the next few years the religious education sky was illuminated by the meteor of Goldmanism. More recently Goldman has suffered from the criticism of religious people that he assumes more symbolism in Bible stories than they are prepared to admit and from psychologists that a developmental study cannot properly be based on a simultaneous study of different children in the various age ranges. There is, moreover, the feeling that his method of questioning his subjects was of a form that was likely to evoke concretistic answers from the younger ones. Nevertheless, his work has been reproduced in extensive form by Peatling in America[6] and by Tamminen in Finland[7] with very similar results. Anyone who wishes to study religious education seriously has to take notice of Goldman's findings, because they do draw attention to two important factors:

(a) that children in the concrete thinking stage (roughly the mental ages of six to twelve) misunderstand symbolic religious statements and take them literally;

(b) that as a result of this they acquire a magical and literalist view of what religion is talking about, and this causes conflict in early adolescence, because their widening experience of the world leads them to think that many incidents in religious stories cannot have happened as they are described. According to Goldman, this conflict between the magicotheological view which they have acquired from their religious education and the logicoscientific view which they are obtaining from their other studies and their experience, causes many to give up thinking seriously about religion from the mental age of ten.

The implication of this seems to be that most of the material that had been taught up to that time in primary schools was unsuitable because it was liable to be misunderstood and because it was causing pupils to reject, rather than understand, religion in the long run. Some re-thinking was needed of the content of religious education in the earlier years, and of how pupils could be helped to deepen and refine their theological concepts in adolescence, so that they did not simply reject their childish view of religion, inadequate though it might be, but deepen it into a more sophisticated and adult one.

One result of Goldman's work was to raise the question of whether it was wise to link religious education so closely to Bible study. His findings showed that extensive use of the Bible with children of all ages was not producing the understanding and commitment that compilers of syllabuses had hoped, and that Biblical material needed much more careful grading to the understanding of the pupils. The equation *Bible Study = Religious Education* was not true, certainly with younger learners.

Hyde's less well known research[8] investigated the relationship between attitude and religious learning in secondary schools. He discovered that a favourable attitude to religion, and to learning about it, was a requisite for retaining the facts imparted in the religious education lesson. Pupils with negative or unfavourable attitudes failed to learn and became progressively less well-disposed, and there were a great many of those. Where there was a favourable attitude, however, learning took place, was remembered, and had the effect of strengthening the positive attitude. The paradox has never been pointed out, but an implication of Hyde's work is that a nation that was, by its laws and syllabuses, requiring its children to be taught Christianity, was, by its abstention from overt religious belief and practice, giving such an unfavourable attitude to religion and religious study as to preclude those requirements being successfully implemented.

These discoveries in the field of the psychology of religious development did not immediately affect thinking about the nature and objectives of religious education. The knowledge that they brought was applied to making the existing type of teaching more effective. It was still thought of as teaching about Christianity, but it tried to achieve success by using material which was more appropriate and more suited to pupils' understanding. Goldman himself wrote: 'Christianity should be taught because it is true . . . and without knowledge of the love of God and a relationship with Him, men and women live impoverished lives'[9] and, for that reason, is called by Schools Council Working Paper 36, *Religious Education in Secondary Schools*,[10] a 'neo-confessionalist'. The *Readiness for Religion* series of lessons[11] for use in primary schools which he edited, where they include religious material, generally have the same sort as is found in the older Agreed Syllabuses. The only difference is that there is less of it.

Furthermore, the revised Agreed Syllabuses which were drawn up in the middle of the 1960s, and claim to have taken the new research findings into account, tend still to express their aims in confessionalist terms. The West Riding Syllabus of 1966 states:

> Expressions of the Christian spirit should be found at many points in the life of the school . . . at the heart of the universe there is a personal God who cares, a spirit who seeks to enter into personal relationship with us . . . Christianity offers standards, not by prescribing rules, but by making people aware of the uniqueness of Jesus and his way of life.

From this, and other similar statements,[12] it seems clear that by that time we had discovered more about how children learn about religion, but had not greatly changed our views of what they should learn and why they should learn it.

At this point, however, new influences begin to affect the

situation, namely the inductive theory of education, the new theology, secularist and humanist pressure, and the increasing presence of immigrants sincerely practising the faiths of the cultures into which they had been born.

The Inductive Theory of Education

There was a time when education was regarded as the authoritarian imparting of facts which the teacher knew and the pupils respectfully accepted. The teacher said, 'This is what there is to know; learn it and you will be educated.' The method worked well with those of good memory and docile temperament, but the inductive theory maintains that wider and deeper learning takes place, and greater insight is achieved, if the children are given appropriate experiences and then encouraged to find out for themselves. On this theory, the teacher says, 'Here are certain experiences available to you; undergo them and find through them what there is to be known.' When such practice became widely used in other subjects, it was natural that there should be a demand for it to be employed in religious education. Some attempt was made to do so, as will be shown below, but there are certain aspects of religion which make it unamenable to such treatment.

Most religions, especially those of the West, tend to have a strong authoritarian element. Their doctrines are frequently claimed to be derived, not from reflections on experience, but from a revelation from a deity, which is self-authenticating and does not need to be verified empirically. In some, a humble acceptance of 'the word of the Lord' is more meritorious than discovering for oneself. This makes religious education a difficult subject for inductive education, particularly when the teacher is a keen believer. The dilemma of teachers trying to teach inductively ideas which are not directly derived from experience, and which they themselves have accepted on other grounds, is discussed in Chapter 4.

The New Theology

What was called 'the new theology' had been growing for some time. Discoveries of how the world worked and how its parts interacted, and attacks by linguistic philosophers on the logical nature of certain religious statements, were causing the old mythologies to crumble. The concept of a God as an entity, 'out there' in space, who had physically created the world, and who maintained a material relationship with it by miracles, avatars and incarnations, was not looking so plausible as formerly. Bultmann had said that God must be sought in the natural, not in the supernatural,[13] and Tillich had said that he must be sought in 'the depth and ground of being'.[14] In England, a book of scholarly essays called *Soundings*[15] had explored these ideas in academic fashion, but they became the subject of popular interest on the publication of J. A. T. Robinson's *Honest to God* in 1963.[16] For the development of thinking about religious education this book was influential in two ways:

(a) it provoked discussion of religion and allowed doubts to be admitted which previously had been suppressed. Many Christian doctrines were expressed in thought forms which were alien to the experience of technological man, but this discrepancy was not recognised publicly. Now that they could be discussed in open debate, those doctrines had to be re-defined if they were to retain credibility. The result was that there no longer seemed to exist a body of doctrine which could be made into a syllabus and taught as accepted truth. Theology had become flexible and a corresponding flexibility entered into religious education. There was also raised the question of what was now to be taught, if the older expressions of belief were abandoned.

(b) perhaps the essence of the new theology was that religion was concerned with the quality of life and not with a non-scientific explanation of the creation and functioning of the universe. Reality, or God, was to be found in the natural, or 'in the depth and ground of being', whatever that might mean. Religion was concerned with values, personal relationships whatever you took 'seriously without any reservation', your 'ultimate concern'. J. A. T. Robinson wrote that a religious question was '*in the first instance* a question about man and not about "God", a word which is becoming increasingly problematic to our generation'.[17] This redefinition of religion suggested what the new content of religious education was to be, namely helping pupils to discover their deepest concern and to think out their personal and social problems in the light of it.

Religious education of this sort had already been suggested by Richard Acland in his book *We Teach Them Wrong* (1963).[18] Acland argued that religious education in primary schools might successfully continue in the way it had always gone because young children are going rapidly through the prior intellectual experience of the human race; consequently, they would accept naturally the older forms of religion, find them apposite to their experience, and not be troubled by the sophisticated doubts of their elders (he wrote before Goldman had demonstrated the difficulties that this sort of teaching occasions for them at the next stage of their development). In the secondary school, however, Acland thought that the continued teaching of doctrine was likely to meet an unfavourable response, and indeed, do damage, and that it should be replaced by an open search for meaning and concern for social situations. He advocates that the name of the subject should be changed to 'Life Discussion Period'.

Loukes took a similar line in his *New Ground in Christian Education*.[19] This book began with a statistical survey of the effect of existing teaching about religion, which showed that the impressions Loukes had recorded in *Teenage Religion* were accurate, and then went on to suggest remedies. Like all education, religious education, for Loukes, was to begin with a 'dialogue about experience', and, moving from the concrete to the abstract, would eventually try to solve the problem of 'What is life for?' From this would follow other questions, such as 'What ought to matter to me?', 'How ought I to live my life?', and so on. All subjects raise these questions to an extent, but religious education should have a unifying influence, being a time set apart to consider the 'religious dimension' of life. The teaching was not to be the promulgation of explicit doctrines but the discovery of values implicit in experience and the becoming aware of this religious dimension to be found in it.

This 'implicit religion approach', as Schools Council Working Paper 36 calls it, set the fashion for much religious education in the next few years. Many teachers continued in the older ways, but those who followed Loukes' advice embarked on the exposition, exploration, and sometimes the solution, of a range of social and moral problems in the hope that, if they delved deeply enough, they would come on religion at the bottom. To the more conservative, religious education seemed to take on the form of moral and social education.

The 'implicit religion' approach enjoyed popularity for a short while, but by 1968 it had begun to wear thin and began to be called in question. There were several reasons for this. Either because teachers were not getting to the religious basis of experience, or because pupils were refusing to, or were incapable of, thinking deeply enough, the 'new religious education' was proving neither more popular nor more successful than the old. Moreover, other school subjects, such as English literature and sociology, were now dealing with the same human problems and children were tiring of a repeated diet of drugs, sex and euthanasia. Other factors, too, had become operative, such as the interest occasioned by the religion of immigrants. It is possible, on reflection, to think that the 'implicit religion' approach had not been given enough time to be tried successfully and that it was abandoned prematurely, but there was a feeling at the time that yet another definition of religious education was needed.

Secularist and Humanist Pressure

When religious education was subjecting itself to a stern self-examination, and candidly confessing its failures in public, as it did in the first half of the 1960s, it was to be expected that those who had no love for it should think the time fitting for an attempt to get rid of it. If it was so ineffective, and so unwanted by the pupils, why spend public money on it? The Humanists and the secularists were not slow to point this out in their own journals and in letters and articles in the educational press.[20] They have so far made little impact in changing the law,[21] although it is possible that they have been influential in getting the subject neglected in schools where head teachers are opposed to religion. On the other hand, public opinion polls which have enquired into parents' wishes have shown a strong majority in favour of retaining the subject,[22] which may account for why there has been no inclination on the part of politicians to consider any modification of the religious clauses of the 1944 Act. None the less, secularist pressure has had three outcomes.

First, it has, paradoxically, enlisted the sympathy of the more thoughtful and open-minded Humanists. This was mostly due to the implicit religion approach, for if religious education was concerned with human problems it was dealing with a field with which Humanism is concerned. This was illustrated by the discussions about religious education that took place between a group of Christians and Humanists at the London University Institute of Education from 1965 onwards, and which produced two pamphlets, written by Howard Marratt and James Hemming, *Religious Education in Schools* and *Humanism and Christianity: the Common Ground on Moral Education*. These showed that responsible Humanists were prepared to accept, and even support, religious education if it could be defined as an open search for meaning and not conducted in a way that they considered antagonistic to their views. In this connection, it is perhaps worth noting that the British Humanist Association (to the chagrin of its more extreme and smouldering members) is now represented on the Religious Education Council of England and Wales.

Secondly, it has aroused an interest in, and demand for, moral education. In the past it had been assumed that moral training was the outcome of religious education, but if the latter was making only intermittent impact pupils were receiving no moral guidance, and the omission ought to be made up some other way. Furthermore, Humanists and secularists, especially those who did not agree with those mentioned in the previous paragraph, interpreted the large parental demand for religious education as, in effect, a request for moral education, and considered that there would be little objection to removing religious education if some kind of training in choice of action were provided in its place. This, coupled with a growing concern about the increase in violence and dishonesty in society at large, evoked an interest in the possibility of an ethical education. The result was the formation of the Social Morality Council, a short-lived Campaign for Moral Education, research programmes into the theory and practice of moral education sponsored by the Schools Council and the Farmington Trust, and the founding of the *Journal of Moral Education*. A discussion of the relationship between religious and moral education occupies Chapter 8.

The third effect of the secularist attack on religious education was to produce a sensitiveness, perhaps an over-sensitiveness, to the danger of indoctrination in religious education. Indoctrination tends to be the teaching of something you don't happen to agree with, and secularists have always regarded religious education in that light. The now openly discussed uncertainty about religious doctrines and the tentative assertions of the new theology, enabled secularists to point out that the doctrines contained in the Agreed Syllabuses were by no means agreed any longer, and that they could not be demonstrated as true, and that to present them as though they were was indoctrination.

To call religious education indoctrination is to call it names rather than contribute to the rethinking of it, but the charge had two results. One was the demand, articulated by Paul Hirst in his article 'Morals, Religion and the Maintained School',[23] that religious education shall confine itself to imparting the facts about religions that are demonstrable and agreed. This seems to remove all the objections at a stroke, but it would mean that the teaching would be confined to statistical statements such as '10% of Cornishmen believe in this doctrine' and 'x% of churches in England are Roman Catholic,' and this will make for dull lessons and promote little understanding of what religion is about. The other result was that, in order to be fair, and to avoid the charge of indoctrination, teachers have tended to be cautious, and so to under-present religious ideas in which they themselves believe. There has been a certain loss of nerve which has affected the way the subject is taught. Every teacher of religious education finds it necessary to protect himself by making a regular public confession that he does not aim to indoctrinate, and some writings on religious education give the impression that the teaching is acceptable provided the pupils never come to any conclusion as a result of it. Perhaps there has been an over-reaction, and teachers have been so afraid of infringing a pupil's religious autonomy that by trying to avoid converting all, they are preventing the reasonable and permissible conversion of any. More thinking seems to be needed as to what indoctrination is and what sort of indoctrination, if any, is permissible in religious education. Chapter 7 is an attempt to contribute to that discussion.

The influence of secularist thinking, and of the general drift away from the 1944 position during the 1960s, is shown by comparing the chapters on religious education in the two official reports issued in that decade, the Newsom Report[24] on secondary modern schools and the Plowden Report[25] on primary schools. In the former, the chapter on 'Spiritual and Moral Development' assumes that the subject will be the transmission of the accepted spiritual ideas and mores of society. Its assumptions are similar to those of the Spens Report[26] issued before the Second World War. The latter, in its majority report, says much the same things, and deprecates that children should be 'confused by being taught to doubt before faith is established'; but it contains a minority report which points out the uncertain nature of religious beliefs and strongly hints that religious teaching has no place in primary schools. This was the first time that a Government-sponsored report had hinted at such things.

The Influence of Immigration

From the middle of the 1960s, reflection on the nature of religious education in England had to take into account the immigrant pupils arriving in the schools. These may have been relatively few in country districts, but in some of the larger cities classes could be found where immigrants formed the majority. Some of them, especially from the West Indies, brought with them a form of Christianity which was less inhibited than that normally found here; others were practising members of non-Christian faiths. Consequently, one might find in a school a number of varieties of Christians, Jews, Sikhs, Muslims and Hindus, as well as the Humanist, the materialist, the active atheist and the apathetic; a sensitive religious education could not ignore this pluralist situation. Some teachers tried to do so, partly because they felt that they had been trained to teach about Christianity and were incompetent to do anything else, partly because they felt that Britain was a Christian country and that it was their duty to explain the Christian basis of Britain's culture to those who had come to live there permanently.

Others, however, saw in the situation an opportunity of widening the content of their teaching and of making a useful contribution to the integration of the immigrants into the community. They saw their task as explaining to their pupils the various religions to be found amongst them, and promoting understanding and tolerance. The aim was to help British-born pupils to understand the religions of their new schoolfellows, and to help the immigrants to understand the religions both of the indigenous population and of each other. Not a few exciting lessons resulted from pupils being encouraged to explain their beliefs to each other, to describe their manners of worship, and to state what their beliefs required of them in the way of conduct. This not only paved the way for the 'phenomenological religious education' that became the fashion subsequently, but it also led to an enriching of the subject and the awakening of a new interest in it.

The pluralistic religious situation in schools accentuated the demand, that had already made itself felt, for the teaching of some kind of comparative study of religion. What had previously been advocated in a desire to be fair, and not to hide from pupils the fact that there were religious reactions to experience other than the Christian, now became more practically possible when there were examples of non-Christian beliefs and practices at hand. What had been a bookish study of the strange ideas and practices of people in remote cultures took on an immediate and practical significance when there was a mosque along the road and a Sikh sitting in the next chair. From this followed an intensified demand for a study of many religions and this began to be provided, even though it involved content which was not included in the Agreed Syllabuses.

One must not assume, however, that by including teaching about the major world religions religious education had escaped all its problems. The assumption that a study of several religions is welcomed by all pupils, meets with understanding on their part, and places the practice beyond the charge of indoctrination, is too facile. Three problems still remain.

Any religion is deeply embedded in the culture from which it springs and an understanding of it requires an equivalent understanding of that culture. Some religions which are now found in England have their cultural basis elsewhere. It is therefore difficult for pupils to understand these faiths before they have studied the cultures from which they have come, and it is rarely possible to do this at satisfactory depth. One may wonder whether a good deal of what has been taught in schools about 'other religions' is a recounting of curiosities rather than a study imparting understanding.

There is, furthermore, the difficulty of teaching about a religion with which one is only externally acquainted. Certainly, teachers do their best to be impartial and no longer follow the former practice of setting up other religions as Aunt Sallys to be knocked down by Christian stones, but it is difficult to avoid unconsciously assessing a religion one does not hold by the criterion of its approximation to one's own and to prevent this assessment influencing one's presentation of it.

The twentieth century mind, with its preoccupation with an empirical and materialistic world view, has reservations about 'spiritual' ideas and difficulties in grasping what religions say about them. These reservations and difficulties are not removed by examining many religions rather than one. Non-empirical ideas which cause difficulty when pupils are asked to consider Christianity, cause the same difficulty when they are encountered in a Buddhist or Islamic setting. Consequently, the introduction of a variety of religions has not solved some of the deepest problems of religious education but moved them into new and wider fields.

In one way, the presence of non-Christian religions in Britain has brought a new problem for religious education. Whereas Christian denominations had ceased to view the teaching of religion in schools as an attempt to convert children to their particular point of view, and there was emerging an opinion that religious education is studying religion rather than creating it and proselytising, certain immigrant communities see it as teaching their faith to their children and are beginning to demand facilities for such in schools. Some are even contemplating building their own schools in which their faith can be taught, and since Church schools are already permitted, there seems no objection to this in principle. If this process goes far it could result in the return of some of the old divisiveness and bitterness, and to the charge that religious education is uneducational because it allows minority groups to indoctrinate with their personal opinions.

Phenomenological Religious Education

As a result of the influences described above and the reservations felt about the 'implicit religion' approach, which seemed to confine the study to a consideration of personal problems and social issues, by 1968 it appeared that the thinking about the nature of the subject had produced much movement but little progress. Its teaching was meeting with no outstanding success and attempts to define its educational aims had led to neither consensus nor clarity. A further assessment seemed needed.

The basis of this reassessment was that schools are educational establishments and that if religious education was to continue in them it had to be justifiable on educational grounds alone.[27] It might produce faith in some and morals in others; it might even be interesting; but unless it was contributing to the educational development of pupils it was taking up time that might be more profitably used. If education is making pupils informedly intelligent about worthwhile topics,[28] then religious education can be included in schools programmes if it is informing pupils about religion, making them discriminating about any form of it they may encounter, and if it can be shown that religion is a worth-while topic of study.

The matter of worth-whileness is crucial, and those who support religious education argue that religion has had, and continues to have, such a formative influence both on culture and on individuals that an educated person needs to know about it and be able intelligently to react to it, even if he himself does not subscribe to any particular form of it. To prove that the subject has no educational value it would be necessary to demonstrate that our culture has entirely cut itself off from any religious influence, and that those who practise it are indulging in an imaginative hobby which has no effect on them at other times and influences neither their character nor their moral choices. If, however, religious beliefs are still influential, a knowledge of what his fellow citizens believe, why they believe it, and the effect of that belief on conduct, would seem part of an educated person's equipment. (See Chapter 9 below.) On such a view, religious education is simply making people educated about religion in all its forms.

This approach to religious education has been called the 'explicit religion'[29] approach, since it is a study of the major explicit forms of religion to be found in the world, and the 'phenomenological' approach. The latter name is borrowed from a method of theological study advocated by certain continental scholars about the beginning of this century. The term 'phenomenology of religion' was coined by the Dutchman P. D. Chantepie de la Saussaye, but the guiding principles of the study were enunciated by Edmund Husserl in his *Logische Untersuchunger* (1900–1).[30]

The essence of this methodology is that you look at religions as an external observer, try to understand what they mean to the believer, but do not raise the question of whether he is wise so to believe, or whether his belief corresponds to truth. Phenomenology is concerned with understanding how a religion is believed and practised and not with deciding whether or not it is true. According to Husserl, the student must bring to his work *epoche* and *eidectic vision*. *Epoche* (from the Greek *epocho*, I hold) means the holding back from any value judgment on what one is studying. One does not criticise the religion under scrutiny from the point of view of one's own apprehensions of truth, and accepts that 'the believer is always right'. *Eidetic vision* (from the Greek *to eidos*, meaning 'that which is seen') is the capacity to see the essence of the phenomena under study, as distinct from what it might have been, or ought to be. In other words, one tries to see the religion whole, to grasp what are the important manifestations of it, and then one stops at that point.

The application of this method of study to education in schools would appear to remove it from accusations of indoctrination or proselytising intention, and was advocated by J. W. D. Smith in his *Religious Education in a Secular Setting*[31] and by Ninian Smart in his *Secular Education and the Logic of Religion*.[32] Smart writes of it thus:

> Religious education could be designed to give people the capacity to understand religious phenomena to discuss sensitively religious claims, to see interrelations between religion and society and so forth.[33]

> Religious education can transcend the informative by being a sensitive induction into religious studies not with the aim of evangelising, but with the aim of creating the capacity to understand and think about religion.[34]

The phenomenological approach is the one that has been chiefly written about and attempted in the recent past and it has provided the underlying philosophy of most of the latest Agreed Syllabuses. At its best, it can be the sensitive induction into thinking about religion that Smart envisaged; often, however, it has been an uninspiring and uncritical imparting of the more obvious facts of the practices of the major world religions. A fuller critique will be undertaken later, but at this stage perhaps one may question whether young children are sophisticated enough to study religion in this way, without asking 'Is it true?'; whether religion seems sufficiently worth-while at present for such study to arouse the interest that enthusiasts for this method of teaching claim; and whether it gives pupils enough help in coming to terms with their own beliefs and in answering some of the philosophical questions that trouble them from time to time.

Changes in Agreed Syllabuses, 1944–1980

Naturally, these fashions in religious education, the confessional, the neo-confessional, the implicit religion approach and the phenomenological study, were not followed by all teachers. Some changed with the times, but others persevered in their old ways, with the result that all these types of teaching can still be seen in schools and a variety of aims can be found in different teachers. A general trend, however, can be observed in the attempts to make religious education responsive to the changing social system and the prevailing forms of thought. A brief survey of the modifications to the Agreed Syllabuses may show this trend.

It is possible to discern five significant changes in the Agreed Syllabuses since they were made a legal requirement.

(a)   The early syllabuses were intended to define the content about which the Churches (that is, the Christian denominations) could reach agreement. The accent was on the word 'agreed'. By setting out that content the syllabuses, almost incidentally, helped the teachers by telling them what to include in their lessons and assuring them that if they kept to the syllabus they would not be liable to give offence or to come under attack, since what they were presenting had agreed public support. As time has passed, denominational agreement has become an almost minimal concern with syllabus makers, and helping teachers to arrive at appropriate lesson content for the children of a secular and pluralist society has appeared much more important. The accent has moved from the word 'agreed' to the word 'syllabus'. This change of emphasis was first apparent in the West Riding of Yorkshire syllabus (1966) which relegated the words 'agreed syllabus' to its sub-title and called itself *Suggestions for Religious Education*.

(b)   Whereas the syllabuses were formerly confined to a study of Christianity, other religions are now included. The Birmingham syllabus of 1975 was the first to establish that world faiths might form part of the study. At secondary level it permits the study of four faiths, one as a major study, and three as minor ones. Christianity must be included, but not necessarily as the major study. This syllabus even goes so far as to permit a pupil to select for a minor study one of the 'stances for living' which 'shares many of the dimensions of religion whilst not admitting belief in realities transcending the natural order',[35] although after legal advice it rather cautiously points out that the purpose of studying a 'life-stance' is to lead to a sharper understanding of religion by providing a contrast. Birmingham having shown that 'other faiths' and 'life-stances' may be part of a legal syllabus, other authorities have followed that lead to varying extents. Some, such as

Avon, Hampshire and Hertfordshire, are thoroughly phenomenological, according equal status to all religions,
whereas others, such as Nottingham and Northampton,
still have a Christian emphasis on the grounds that the
Christian religion has made the greater contribution to our
culture.

(c)   The machinery for making the syllabuses has often been
used flexibly in the last decade. Earlier, the Agreed Syllabus Conferences, with their theological, ecclesiastical and
local authority representation, did the major work of
selecting and arranging the teaching content. Latterly,
they have been willing to allow working groups of teachers
to undertake such tasks. In some counties the teacher
groups have prepared the syllabus almost entirely and the
conference has done no more than accept formally and
approve their work on behalf of the Churches and local
authority. In other places, however, county councillors
(rather than churchmen) have been known to use the
syllabus conference to try to inform teachers what it is
their duty to teach, even though their demands, sometimes based on comparative ignorance of modern education and of how contemporary children think, have been
unrealistic. Flexible though they have been on occasions,
one must question whether the provisions for making
Agreed Syllabuses, intended, as they were, for a different
social, theological and educational age, ought to remain
unmodified.

(d)   Following from greater teacher involvement, recent syllabuses have recognised that teachers need freedom to select
precisely what they are to teach at any particular time.
Local conditions, the needs and interest of the pupils,
their previous education and background, the availability
of illustrative material and similar considerations, all influence the selection of lesson content for sensitive
teachers. Syllabuses, such as those of Birmingham, Avon
and Hampshire, have tried to give teachers that freedom
by not presenting a detailed description of lesson content,
broken down into ages and years and terms, but merely
specifying appropriate aims and objectives for broadly
defined age groups, and passing on to the teachers the
responsibility of selecting materials which will help them
to achieve those objectives. The purpose of these brief

statements of the aims of the subject (the Birmingham syllabus proper occupies only four pages) is to define the subject and to give it some coherence after the rapid changes that have affected it in the immediate past. Unlike their predecessors, these newer syllabuses are not defining areas of agreement between religious bodies but trying to say what is an appropriate religious education for children of the pluralist society.

One difficulty of the new type of syllabus is that it assumes a competence and an originality that not all teachers possess. It is possible for such syllabuses to give too little guidance to hard-pressed teachers in making lessons in what is a difficult and sometimes contentious subject. Local authorities that have made aim-orientated rather than content-orientated syllabuses have recognised this by making supplementary handbooks or packs of teaching materials to make good the deficiency.

(e) There is a strong contrast between the older and the newer syllabuses in what is suggested for primary school children, especially in the initial years. The warnings of Goldman about the difficulty that young children have in understanding theological material are being influential and the implicit religious approach is largely used. Instead of Bible-based study, the syllabuses prescribe an investigation into the children's surroundings and relationships, similar to what is undertaken in primary schools under general education. It is not always made clear why this counts as 'religious education' and more thinking needs to be done about the connection between this part of the syllabus and the more specific study of religions that is required later.[36]

One way of appreciating how religious education itself and the syllabuses that define it have been modified in response to the social, intellectual and educational changes since 1944, is to compare the way in which their aims are set out in their various preambles. The following is a selection:

Cambridgeshire Syllabus (1949)
The aim must be to lead children to an experience of God, His Church, and His Word, an experience based on worship, fellowship and service.

Lincolnshire Syllabus (1964)
The syllabus is deliberately designed as an evangelistic influence . . . the aim is to lead pupils to a personal knowledge of Jesus Christ.

West Riding of Yorkshire Syllabus (1966)
Personal needs are religious needs which are only satisfied by the growing discovery that at the heart of the universe there is a God who cares.

Birmingham Syllabus (1975)
The syllabus should be used to enlarge pupils' understanding of religion by studying world religions and by exploring all those elements in human experience which raise questions about life's ultimate meaning and value.

Hampshire Syllabus (1978)
It is no part of the responsibility of a county school to promote any particular religious standpoint, neither can an exclusive Christian content do justice to the nature of the subject.

Northamptonshire Syllabus (1980)
Religious Education . . . is most appropriately seen as an introduction to an individual's religious quest and some of its contemporary expressions in belief and practice rather than a process of induction into a particular religious tradition. The pursuit of such an aim is designed to help pupils to identify for themselves the fundamental questions of human existence, so that they may continue to reflect upon these and arrive at the decisions life calls for in a responsible way.

The quotations show how religious education at present is not thought of as giving pupils religious certainties but as helping them to act responsibly in an age of religious uncertainty. Behind this is the conviction that an intelligent reaction to experience involves the facing of certain fundamental problems and that beliefs, whether they are theistic or naturalistic, affect the solution of such problems. Some understanding of the effect of beliefs and some appreciation of one's own beliefs are therefore necessary. How the teaching should be organised to help pupils acquire those skills will be discussed in the third section of this book. Before then, it will be necessary to look at certain outstanding problems which have to be faced before a theory of religious education for a questing world can be fashioned.

NOTES

1   Institute of Christian Education (1957).
2   University of Sheffield (1961).
3   H. Loukes (1961).
4   Ibid., p. 93.
5   The findings are fully set out in R. J. Goldman (1964).
6   John H. Peatling, 'On beyond Goldman', in *Learning for Living*, 16, 3, Spring 1977.
7   Kalevi Tamminen, 'Research concerning the development of religious thinking in Finnish students', in *Character Potential: A Record of Research*, 6, 4, February 1974.
8   Reported in K. E. Hyde (1965).
9   R. J. Goldman (1965).
10   Schools Council (1971).
11   Published by Rupert Hart-Davis, London, 1965–6.
12   E.g., the Cornwall Agreed Syllabus (1964) states, 'For the purpose of this syllabus, Religious Education is a term which takes for granted the Christian religion, not because we find none of God's truth in other creeds but because we believe we find all God's truth in Jesus Christ.'
13   In his *Jesus Christ and Mythology* (1958).
14   'The name of this infinite and inexhaustible depth and ground of all being is *God*. That depth is what the word God means.' (Tillich, 1962, p. 63.)
15   A. R. Vidler (ed.) (1962).
16   J. A. T. Robinson (1963).
17   J. A. T. Robinson (1965).
18   R. Acland (1963).
19   H. Loukes (1965).
20   E.g. Brigid Brophy, *Religious Education in State Schools*. Fabian Society Tract 374. Fabian Society, London, 1967.
21   The British Humanist Association put forward detailed suggestions for the reform of the legislation relating to religion in schools in its tract *Objective, Fair and Balanced* in 1975.
22   *New Society*, 5, 139, May 1965, records one such poll. P. May summarises the findings of the investigation, which he and O. R. Johnston had conducted, in *Learning for Living*, 6, 4, 1966. The opinions of the parents of sixth form grammar school students are set out in E. Cox (1967).
23   Reprinted in C. Macy (1969).
24   Ministry of Education, *Half Our Future*, H.M.S.O., 1963.
25   Department of Education and Science, *Children and their Primary Schools*, H.M.S.O., 1967.

26   Board of Education, *Secondary Education with special reference to Grammar Schools and Technical High Schools*, H.M.S.O., 1938.

27   See E. Cox, 'Educational religious education', in E. Lord and C. Bailey (1973).

28   cf. R. S. Peters in his *Ethics and Education* (Peters, 1966, p. 35): 'Education . . . involves the intentional transmission of what is worth-. while.'

29   In Schools Council Working Paper 36 (note 10 above).

30   For a brief outline of phenomenology see the article by E. Sharpe, 'The phenomenology of religion', in *Learning for Living*, 15, 1, Autumn 1975.

31   J. W. D. Smith (1969).

32   N. Smart (1968).

33   Ibid., p. 96.

34   Ibid., p. 97.

35   City of Birmingham, *Agreed Syllabus of Religious Instruction*, 1975, p. 8.

36   Chapter 3 below is an attempt to initiate such thinking.

The Problems

3 The Problem of what to Teach in the Primary School

The researches, mentioned in the previous chapter, into the development of religious thinking in young children have drawn attention to the difficulties occasioned by the misunderstandings of religious language and stories that occur in the early years of schooling. Metaphorical expressions are likely to be taken literally, parables and myths likely to be confused with historical narratives. Young children seem easily to get the wrong ideas if presented with doctrinal and other religious forms of expression which demand a sophisticated response to reveal their full meaning.

It is possible for too much to be made of this and that young children can benefit more deeply than is often supposed from myth and fantasy, provided it is presented to them sensitively. This is an area where further investigation is urgently needed. Furthermore, teachers tell of their young pupils earnestly making religious statements, which they may not fully understand, in order to please, and finding pleasure in stories from the Bible and other sacred literature, stories of miracles and theophanies, which they may well question at a later age. The matter is complicated by the fact that the attitudes and moral teaching of the stories do have an influence on conduct which can persist even when the stories themselves have been scornfully rejected in early adolescence. Thus it would appear that a traditional type of religious education can be given in primary schools with some success, though at the expense of causing difficulties subsequently. The question is whether children should be deprived of these early joyful experiences of religious stories, and primary school teachers denied what seems a success, in the interests of fuller intellectual development at a later date.

Moreover, the newer syllabuses define religious education in terms of skills in understanding religions, of appreciating what different people believe and how their beliefs are expressed in their behaviour and life styles, of ability to use religious language, and of awareness of one's own beliefs and commitments. These skills and perceptions require some experience of life and some developed mental ability. Older pupils may bring these attributes to the study, but children in infant and junior schools probably cannot. How, then, does one deal with religious education in early school years?

The work of the Schools Council Primary Schools Religious Education Curriculum Development Project at Lancaster University has gone some way to answering that question, and teachers have reacted warmly to its *Discovering an Approach*,[1] with its many imaginative suggestions for classroom procedures. Its rationale, however, could be made more explicit, and there may be some advantage in considering further what it is wise to attempt in religious education with children who have not yet the mental capacity or length of experience to react to religion in its fullness, and of how their learning relates to what they may be able to undertake when they get older.

It can be argued that religious education ought not to be included in the primary school curriculum, that, like sex and rugby football, it is not appropriate for the very young. On the other hand, what is undertaken in the early formative years will influence the attitude of pupils to the study when they can reasonably embark on it. More important, there may be certain learning and certain awareness that need to be acquired at an early stage if religious education is going to seem either worthwhile or intelligible later on.

The major part of religious education in the first school years would seem at present to consist either of simple Christian exercises, such as hearing Bible stories and indulging in hymns and prayers thought appropriate to childish understanding, or of a study of the more obvious religious phenomena, such as what happens at Christian festivals, how Muslims celebrate Ramadan, what Jews do at Hanukkah, how sacred buildings are equipped and what objects of worship are used in them. This is thought to be good for children, or to help them to understand their culture and their neighbours, or to lead them, through examination of simple religious externals, to an understanding of how religious people believe and feel. Certainly, it increases their knowledge (of an area of human activity with which many of them have had minimal contact and in which they have no intention of ever participating), but one wonders whether it has much effect beyond that, and it often seems to be a learning about the curious activities that remote groups practise. The later development of pupils' understanding of religion may demand that they be given something different from this, and something that does not, at first glance, seem closely connected with what is traditionally thought of as religion. Just as learning to count may seem remote from understanding the theory of relativity, yet is a necessary step towards that understanding, so certain skills and presuppositions, which do not in themselves seem closely connected with religion, may have to be acquired as a prerequisite to the study of religion at a later age.

To put it another way, in order to read one has first to recognise patterns of letters; to engage in mathematical calculations one has to have number sense; to study music adequately one has to have a sense of interval, pitch, key and rhythm. Unless these primary awarenesses are developed, one cannot 'do' the subject. What needs to be developed before one can 'do' religion?

There are a number of basic awarenesses without which religious study is impossible and apparently futile. For want of a better term, I propose to call these awarenesses 'sensitivities', though readers must be warned that I am using the word in a special way, as a technical term, and not in its usual or its psychological meaning.

There would seem to be at least six of these basic awarenesses or sensitivities:

1 *A sense of the mystery inherent in life.* The fact that anything exists at all, that matter behaves as it does, that it evokes in the observer feelings of wonder (and sometimes of awe and dread) can lead to this sense of mystery. A feeling of it, and a response to it, is perhaps one of the mainsprings of religions, which refer to it, in its most intense forms, as 'the numinous', or 'the sense of the sacred'. Those who say that they do not feel it, or that it is an illusion, usually find religious responses to existence to be incomprehensible.

2 *A sense of continual change.* By this is meant an awareness that nothing in human experience is static and that everything is changing and passing. The natural world is in a constant state of flux, we ourselves are transitory, and friendships and personal relationships are ever reorganising themselves into

new patterns. The world will never again be as it is at this
moment. By the next moment it will be changed, and human
beings have to learn to live with and come to terms with (and
accept and contribute to) this kaleidoscope. Heracleitus,[2]
who made the concept of impermanence the basis of his
philosophophy in describing this universal flux, wrote, 'You
cannot step twice into the same river, for fresh waters are ever
flowing in upon you.' A more recent writer, Neville Cardus,
called it 'Time's magical vanishings', and thought that those
who are unaware of it or indifferent to it 'go through life
spiritually half deaf or myopic'.[3]

3 *A sense of our relationship to, and dependence on, the natural
   order.* Human beings are physically part of the animal king-
   dom and they rely for their food on the process of growth in
   other animals and in plants. It is true that, having come to the
   stage of foresight and invention, man has been able, to an
   extent, to cut himself off from his surroundings, to exploit
   the environment to his advantage, and by means of storage
   and refrigeration to protect himself temporarily from its
   fluctuations. This has recently led to a preoccupation with
   invention at the expense of foresight, with a consequent
   dislocation of the ecological system which could, at its most
   extreme, place the human race in jeopardy. That shows how
   the human race is still ultimately related to, and reliant upon,
   the natural order of which it is a part and on which it
   ultimately depends. This awareness may be overemphasized
   in natural religion and underemphasized in the more sophisticated and theological faiths, but it is probably one of the
   fundamental responses to life from which religious feelings
   emerge.

4 *A sense of order in what we experience.* By this I mean an
   apprehension that the world in which we live and the experiences that come to us in it can be understood. The things that
   go on around us are reliable and consistent and can be reacted
   to in a rational manner. The whole is not an unrelated chaos.
   This awareness lies behind the examination of the world in a
   scientific manner and the modification of it by technology. It
   leads to the conviction that life too can be understood and
   may have some point. One is not maintaining here that there
   is some obvious overall purpose that we can easily discern and
   call 'the will of God'. That is part of the superstructure that

developed religions build up on this sensitivity. Such purpose may or may not exist; we may or may not be able to have some inkling of what it is.[4] Those are the considerations that religions deal with. What one is arguing is that unless a person has the underlying feeling that the world has some kind of order, however dimly perceived, the questions of purpose that religions are concerned with will not seem worth discussing, and religions will not seem worth taking seriously.

5 *A realisation that there are other persons in the universe* and that they deserve consideration and respect. Although I have to look at the world through my own eyes, I am not the centre of it, nor am I the only person in it. There are other centres of consciousness, other individuals, and I have to take them and their ideas and feelings into account. Just as I have to relate to the whole of the natural environment, so I have to relate to these individuals, but in a special way, because they also are living, feeling, thinking, rejoicing and suffering. Our interpersonal relationships influence that thinking, feeling and suffering. We live in a complex of individuals and greatly mould and fashion each other. Recognition of this leads to an appreciation of our own personal position in society and to an awareness of the moral questions of how others ought to be respected and treated.

6 *A sense of right and wrong.* This last sensitivity follows from the one previously described, and is an awareness that perhaps actions can be divided into those that are desirable and good, and those that are undesirable and bad, and that there ought to be some way of deciding into which particular category any particular action can be placed. This may not be a fully developed moral sense, which is able to classify every action without hesitation, but a hunch that there are moral choices to be made, even if they are difficult and the criteria for them not immediately apparent. Without that hunch moral search will seem meaningless and unnecessary.

These six would seem to be examples of the sensitivities that underlie a religious response to experience. Unless a person has some of them, and is conscious of having them, religions will seem to be irrelevant activities, and the study of religions will be reduced to a pastime. Perhaps it is worth while pointing out here that modern industrialised urban society tends to dull these sensitivities. An entirely man-made environment, where the origin of everything in sight can be described in mechanical terms, tends to reduce the sense of mystery;[5] manufactures and warehouses help to remove the awareness of change and of dependence on environment; industrial and political rivalry and class competition lessen respect for individuals (one doesn't respect the other rats in the race); and the urge to affluence and success can dull the sense of right and wrong. The overlaying of these basic sensitivities may be the reason why religions (except in their more *outré* form) flourish less in industrialised societies. If so, it is necessary in the educational system of such societies for more time to be given in schools to the development of those sensitivities if religious education is to be, and be seen to be, a worth-while activity.

The development of these sensitivities may be the beginning of religious education, but it is not the whole of it. To see how it leads on to what is done at later ages, we have to explore the link between the basic sensitivities and developed forms of religion. The sensitivities raise, in those who have them, certain questions and emotions. The questions include: Why are things here? What is the explanation, if any, of this mystery? What, if any, is the explanation of this continual change? What is the purpose of our interplay with the surrounding universe and with each other? How do we decide which actions are right and which are wrong? Does any of this complex experience 'make sense', or is the idea of 'making sense' something that we foist on an inexplicable universe? Furthermore, there are the emotions of fear, apprehension, wonder, dread, and affection that often accompany these questions. In addition, there are the related feelings of conscience, and the problems of how to resolve the tensions that a sensitive approach to life and its environment brings.

From a practical point of view, religions can be seen as formal ways of attempting to answer those questions and of dealing with those emotions. Their doctrines try to explain why the world is as it is and why the human race is constituted as it is. Other ideologies or life-stances do similarly. The religions base their explanations on belief in the existence of a supernatural original power, which they call god. The other ideologies, which prefer not to be called 'religious', discern the answers to the questions in something more material, something within creation itself. Some persons belong to neither camp and settle the questions by denying that they are worth asking, or that any answer to them is possible. The point being made is that religions and ideologies are concerned with the questions that are raised by the sensitivities described above and that those without the sensitivities will fail to appreciate that concern. The religious go further than the non-religious ideologies in that they, through their worship and ceremonies, attempt to provide a way of coping with the emotions, the apprehensions and fears that the sensitivities evoke.

It may be true to say that, on this view, religions are a set of second order statements. The sensitivities are primary, and the way religions deal with their questions and emotions is secondary. The history of religions, however, shows that it is very easy for the connection between the two to be forgotten, so that the doctrines, the rites and the ceremonies of religion become cut off from the sensitivities, the questions and the emotions and so appear arbitrary, formal, groundless, and, consequently, an in-game, a hobby of the initiated, rather than a serious attempt to deal with something deep in human experience. For instance, it seems reasonable to think that the Christians began singing the Benedicite in their worship because it seemed to give expression to the emotions evoked by their sensitivity to the mystery and change in the environment and their response to it. But if the practice and the sensitivities become divorced, Christians can give the impression that religion is singing the Benedicite on Sunday mornings in the proper way at the proper seasons whether one feels the need to do so or not. Religion when it reaches this stage, becomes a matter of holding the approved beliefs and indulging in the approved ceremonies, and can be formalised behaviour rather than a deep response to living.

A study of the history of most religions usually reveals periods when the religion had lost contact with its essential sensitive attitude to experience and become a stereotyped formality. Amos protested that the Hebrew religion of his time had suffered that fate and had become a matter of meticulously conducted 'solemn feasts' which had little to do with genuine piety.[6] It is possible to see Jesus' controversies with the orthodox Judaism of his day as a protest against its stereotyping and its formality. A case can be made out for regarding the Reformation as partly a similar protest in Christian history. More germane to our purpose is the possibility that many religions have reached a similar state at the present time, and are, to a fairly large extent, concerned with the adherence to a number of doctrines and the indulgence in certain practices which are only rarely and obviously connected with the feelings and emotions that gave rise to them in the first place. That may be why religions are judged by many to be a kind of fantasy or a game without close relevance to the raw business of living.

If that is so, when we come to teach about religions in schools, we may be doing something which may well not seem particularly vital to the learners once they have got beyond the trustful wondering of early childhood. To teach about second order doctrines and second order practices without reference to the basic sensitivities that underlie them will seem unrelated to the pupil's experiences and consequently relatively unimportant. That may explain why pupils' attitudes to the religious education lesson becomes progressively unfavourable during their time at school, changing from the earnest interest of the early years to the hesitating reservations of upper junior and lower secondary ages and the often angry and scornful rejection of adolescence.

One of the problems of religious education teachers is how to overcome that deterioration of attitude and maintain pupils' interest as they mature. If I have been right in arguing that religion springs from the sort of sensitivities described above, and that a study of religion will not seem a worth-while activity to those in whom those sensitivities are not developed, then one of the ways of making the study of religion seem important, worth undertaking, would be first to cultivate those awarenesses. Perhaps we should be dealing with them in the first years of schooling,[7] rather than trying to teach about developed doctrines and practices, which, as the Plowden Report pointed out,[8] are beyond the comprehension of the very young.

It may be argued that children have these sensitivities anyway, because they are innate. Certainly, they seem to be latent in children, but they need to be developed and fortified against the tendency (noted above) for modern urban life to stunt them. They can easily be overlaid and forgotten unless something is done to train them. Such training would seem to involve three stages.

i   Firstly, the attention of children can be drawn to the fact that they feel those sensitivities. This means making them consciously aware of the mystery and the change around them, and of their relationship with other people and with things. Much of the primary school curriculum is already doing this, though not necessarily calling it religious education, by exploring the world and human senses and human relationships. It helps children to look at the world through its

projects, its nature tables, its investigation of the neighbourhood and its experiments with the use of basic materials.
Religious education at this stage may not be a clearly dif-
ferentiated activity, but it may still have a contribution to
make. Its peculiar concern may be to draw attention, in an
unsentimental, uncomplex and matter-of-fact way, to the
manner in which the discovery of the nature of the world has
implications. It is not merely a matter of learning what is
there. For that knowledge points to certain things to be
thought about, certain things to be wondered at, certain
things to be related to, and certain problems to be solved.
These are matters that will have to be considered as pupils
grow older.

2 Secondly, the sensitivities, having been noticed, will need to
be cultivated. They do not grow on their own without use. In
cultivating them, the religious education teacher is able to
relate his subject to those parts of the curriculum that deal
with the arts. The poet, the writer, the musician, the artist, all
have their sensitivities to creation highly developed and are
trying, in their various art forms, to express what they feel.
Those who read their writings, listen to their music and react
to their paintings, are enabled to see the world through the
eyes of the artist and join him in his percipient response to it.
Therefore, religious education may be linked at all times, but
particularly in the early years, with reading poetry, with
producing free writing, with listening to and making music,
and with drama, paintings, collages and so on. Such activities, by developing sensitiveness to the problems and emotions of living, are contributing, not all that indirectly, to the
development of the understanding of religion, even though
doctrines and religious ceremonies are not mentioned. Such
procedure may not turn out copper-bottomed Christians,
Buddhists, Humanists or what have you, but they are prepar-
ing pupils for a more cognitive examination of religions when
they are intellectually equipped to undertake such study.

3 The third stage is helping pupils to appreciate how religions
are ways of answering the questions evoked by those sensitivities, and a means of regulating the emotions they arouse.
This is a more academic study of religions, and probably
belongs to the late years of primary schooling and the secondary years. There is not much point in drawing attention to,

and cultivating, the sensitivities that are necessary before you can 'do' religion and then not actually going on to do it. This means investigating the relationship between the sensitive awarenesses that we have been cultivating and the pronouncements and practices of religious people. The teacher has now to say to his students, 'Let us try to understand what religions are saying by their doctrines, their myths, their stories, their ceremonies, and how this links up with, and springs from, what we have been studying in school in other ways.' It is possible that this important link has been underemphasized in existing religious education syllabuses. There has been a tendency for primary schools to cultivate the necessary sensitivities and for secondary schools to embark on a cognitive study of religious dogmas, moral theories, and worship, without making pupils aware of the relation between the two. Unless they appreciate that the doctrines are ways of answering the questions previously raised, that the ceremonies are formal ways of expressing and channelling the emotions felt, and that the myths are ways of coming to an appreciation of our values and intentions, which a sensitive reaction to experience has distilled, then religious study can readily seem an irrelevant and arbitrarily imposed task.

Though they do not explicitly admit to it, the recent Agreed Syllabuses seem to have had in mind a theory not dissimilar from that set out in this chapter. In the early years of schooling they provide for little specific religious teaching, but recommend exploration of the nature of the self and of human abilities, of the relationship with family, friends, neighbours, and so on, and of the nature and care of things in the environment. This has led to some confusion among primary school teachers, who tend to react in one of two ways. Recognising that their previous practice of confining religious education to the telling of Bible stories (for which they had been trained and frequently did excellently) was not entirely appropriate to the present situation, some have enthusiastically adopted the new syllabuses and felt liberated by 'no longer having to do religious education', while others have wondered whether they are failing in their duty because they see no 'religious' content in what the newer syllabuses prescribe. If both parties could look on their work, and on the newer syllabuses, as concerned with developing the sensitivities which, as argued above, are a prerequisite to understanding the purpose of religious beliefs and ceremonies, the confusion that sometimes appears to exist about the scope and objectives of primary school religious education would be lessened, and the teaching would have a more defensible purpose. It could no longer be accused of being sentimental story-telling with a view to premature indoctrination.

Explicit Teaching about Religion in Primary Schools

From what has been written above, it might appear that explicit teaching about the phenomena of religion will not be required in the primary school, that there we concentrate on developing wonder and a sense of change and order and relationships, while leaving the study of religious doctrines and practices to the secondary school. But young children will be coming into contact with religion, even in a secular world, and there are two areas in particular in which explicit teaching may be desirable. Firstly, they will encounter religious festivals, Christmas and Easter, and in some places Diwali, Hanukkah, Passover, and so on, as well. Furthermore, they may find their families involved in *rites de passage*, baptism, bar mitzvah and bat mitzvah, religious marriage and burial ceremonies and the like. Some teaching about the outward forms of these ceremonies and a glimpse of their significance is needed to help pupils understand what is going on around them. Secondly, the better known stories from sacred literature are still closely bound up in our culture. Young children enjoy these stories, as stories, often find them fascinating, and do not seem to be troubled by the questions of veracity and credibility that concern adults. In British culture, the majority of these stories come from the Christian and Jewish scriptures, but other sacred literature is increasingly contributing, and, carefully chosen, these tales should perhaps be told in the primary school as part of cultural training.

In the past, the reading of scripture and the learning about religious ceremonies has often made up the whole of the primary school religious education syllabus and there are those who still think it sufficient. It is not suggested here that such study should be abandoned, but that an unrelieved diet of it may be producing religious nausea in children by the time of the end of their primary school experience. By then, religious ceremonies and stories seem to have been learned but not understood or accepted, because of an over-literal interpretation of them. The solution may not be to abandon the diet entirely but to add something to it that will make it more assimilable. It is possible that pupils may be more apt to see the significance for believers of religious language and behaviour if the study of scriptures and ceremonies is interspersed with the sensitivity training described above, and then the link made between the two. The object would be to encourage pupils to a realisation that the stories and the practices are the ways in which believers deal with the questions and emotions that arise from the sense of wonder, change, relationship and order that they themselves feel. They may not wish to respond that way themselves, but they may understand better why other people do. Without that appreciation, religious stories and customs can appear empty and foolish and not worth thinking about further. But if the possibility is raised that there may be something in them, the way is opened for the secondary school teacher to ask, 'What is the deeper meaning of religious talk and action? What do they mean to those who indulge in them?'

NOTES

1   Schools Council (1977).
2   An Ephesian philosopher who lived 540–475 B.C. He wrote in Greek, and his views are summed up in the phrase *panta rei*, 'all things are changing'.
3   Neville Cardus, *Full Score* (1970).
4   Those who have decided that the universe is purposeless, or that the idea of purpose is something that we project upon it, find religion, with its search for, or assertion of, purpose, a futile activity. But that decision is just as much a matter of faith as belief in God or in purpose.
5   Illustrated at length in Una Ellis-Fermor's *Masters of Reality* (1941).
6   Amos 5, 21–4.
7   This is not something that is done in the early years and finished with. Sensitivity cultivation is part of religious education at all stages, but it may be strategically wise to concentrate on it in primary schools.
8   In its minority report.

4 Problems of Commitment

All school subjects involve commitments. The history teacher will not make much progress unless his classes have an initial commitment to the study of history, and he hopes by his lessons to reinforce and extend that commitment. A music teacher attempts to foster a commitment to indulge in, and respond to, music making; the object of health education is to produce a commitment to *mens sana in corpore sano*, and one could go on similarly through all the disciplines. Religious education is even more deeply concerned with this, since it is a study of how men and women have accepted deep commitments to what they conceive to be the truth about experience and of how they feel that truth has some claim upon their loyalty and their actions. Furthermore both teachers and pupils have their own obligations to what they conceive to be ultimately important, which can influence both the presentation of the lesson by the teacher and the response to it by the learner. Such commitment in both teachers and learners can cause peculiar problems.

Religions, with some reason, describe their adherents' convictions as truths arrived at, and held by, faith. The believer says, 'These are ideas which I take to be true, this is the secret of experience, this is what the world and life is about, and, as a consequence, I think I am committed to behave in such and such a way.' This truth cannot, however, be empirically demonstrated, otherwise it could quickly be transmitted to all thinking people, the problems of religious pluralism would be solved, and all could embrace the one true, universal religion. Instead this 'truth' is held as a faith or a conviction, and the believer sees it differently from the unbeliever. To the former it is truth, in the light of which he lives; to the latter it is at best an hypothesis and at worst an illusion.

It would make religious education easier if we knew more than
we do about how commitments are arrived at by the individual.
Some seem to come to them by accepting the beliefs of the
community in which they are brought up, particularly when the
community is homogeneous in its beliefs and practices, and
questions about them and about alternative beliefs are not often
asked. Others seem to come on their commitments as the result of
some personal, deep, transcendental experience. This can be very
intense, as in the case of the great religious innovators, Jesus,
Muhammad, Siddhartha Gautama, say. Recent writings, such as
those of Michael Paffard in *Inglorious Wordsworths*[1] and Edward
Robinson in *The Original Vision*,[2] suggest that a less intense, and
often fleeting, form of a transcendental experience is widespread,
particularly in childhood and early adolescence. Those who have
felt it describe it as a very personal experience, almost impossible
to communicate to others or to discuss, but formative of a
philosophy of life or a world view or a religious commitment.
Whether it is interpreted in a religious or a non-religious sense
depends on the cultural background and the vocabulary of the
experiencer.

> An experience which one writer may describe as a revelation of,
> or communion with, God appears on the evidence of his words
> to be identical with what another writer will call an ecstatic kind
> of aesthetic joy: identical, that is, apart from the interpretation
> he puts on it. The absence or presence of a theistic gloss seems to
> be very much a matter of the writer's background or beliefs.[3]

Whatever its origin, religious commitment (or faith) may be
held in either a hard or a soft form. In its hard form the believer
avers that he has grasped certain ultimate unchangable truths,
which have come to him through an unquestionably authentic
experience, or been revealed to him by an unquestionable source,
and that he must live in the light of those truths without swerving,
and that even to doubt them, or to consider that other views might
have any element of veracity, is disloyal and therefore unthink-
able. It is possible to defend this view, to an extent, on the grounds
that if one has come on what seems to be the truth one must think
that those who claim to have found another or contradictory way of
expressing truth are in error, but it can quickly lead to fanaticism,
and it has been the source of intolerance, religious wars and
persecutions. The soft form of commitment occurs when the
believer considers that he has made a serious attempt to grasp the

truth, but that the way it appears to him is relative to his experience and culture rather than compellingly and demonstrably proven. On this view every individual has to work out to the best of his ability what he thinks is true and live according to it until such time as further experience or deeper insight suggest the need for modification. To put it colloquially, he says, 'This is the best that I can do, in the circumstances, to find out what ultimately matters, and I'm going to respond to it sincerely, but not pigheadedly. If ever I come to think that I have been mistaken, I will change. Moreover, I recognise that others are doing similarly, and I have to respect their views, in so far as they are honestly acquired, even if I do not agree with them.' As one would expect, these two ways of looking at religious commitment lead to widely differing views of religious education.

There is another type of conviction which is affecting religious education. It may be wrong to call it a conviction, since it is a revulsion, often emotional, against all manifestations of religious experience. Sometimes because of past intolerances and conflicts between religions, sometimes because of the identification of particular religious organisations with class and social privileges, sometimes because of the unsympathetic and authoritarian way religion was taught to them in schools, many have an emotional, unanalysed set against religion and are embarrassed when it is mentioned. They either try to ignore it or they get aggressive against it, regarding it as an aberration of the human race out of which we should now grow when we have other, more publicly demonstrable, ways of apprehending truth and coming on a rational philosophy of life. Such a conviction is unlikely to be found among teachers of religious education, but they have to take into account how it will be affecting the attitudes of some of the pupils and conditioning the reactions of certain colleagues and educational administrators.

These attitudes to religious commitment, the hard, the soft, and the sceptical, will be found in pupils and in teachers and they need to be taken into account in devising a strategy for religious education.

Pupils' Commitments

Pupil commitment is unlikely to be influencing learning to any great extent in the primary school. Children there have not lived long enough to have formed deep and definite commitments.

They are still exploring the nature of the world and becoming conscious of their reaction to it and this may lead to commitment later on. Perhaps at this stage religious education should be encouraging that exploration and drawing attention to the possibility of searching for meaning in experience, without any preconceived notions of what commitments the search will eventually produce.

In the secondary schools, however, there will be a small number of hardline believers, often associated with particular sects, such as Jehovah's Witnesses, Plymouth Brethren, Rastafarians, and others. There may be a larger number of sceptics who have caught from their elders a scorn of all religious ideas, which they hold too childish to be worthy of serious consideration. There will be others who have recently undertaken a formal act of religious commitment, such as confirmation or bar mitzvah or bat mitzvah, which, even when initially embarked upon for social or cultural reasons, will have raised religious questions in their minds. Similar questions may also be occurring to pupils who belong to none of these categories.

This mixture of commitments and incipient commitments will be found in almost all classrooms outside schools with a specific religious affiliation, and the teacher must consequently expect the teaching to meet with differing reactions and differing understandings. The sceptics will put up automatic resistance unless they can be shown that the study has a rationale and a purpose other than persuading them to believe the unbelievable. They have to be assured that it is worth their interest and that it has something of value to say to them before they will listen. The hardline believers will respond freely to lessons which concern their own faiths but will incline to be impatient when the teacher is dealing with other beliefs or discussing questions of meaning. They will welcome a dogmatic type of teaching which will be repulsive to all the others. The questioners, who recognise that a belief system of some sort is desirable, and possibly inescapable, but who have not yet decided where they personally stand, will welcome liberal discussion and be prepared to study a variety of religious beliefs in the hope that they may find, through that study, some help in defining their own commitments. They may not, however, find it easy to appreciate the certainty with which religious people talk about their tenets, and if the teaching is over-authoritarian they may react unfavourably and join the sceptics.

How is the teacher to deal with these multifarious responses to his work? He can decide to concentrate on those whose commitments correspond to his own and who are thereby able to listen and react favourably, accepting that he can do nothing for the others. Alternatively he can try to communicate with all in a way that will help them. What would this more difficult course involve? Probably the number of pupils in entrenched positions, whether sceptics or hardline believers, is small. Most adolescents, if one can talk with them and get their confidence, are prepared to discuss ultimate questions and anxious to discover some theory of living. They are curious about what religious people mean when they talk about 'God', about why they believe in God, about how they envisage him, and about what sort of obligations that belief entails. But the answers that formal religions give to those questions seem unsatisfying. Furthermore, if Robinson and Paffard are correct, many of the pupils will have had a transcendental experience which they will wish to take into account in fashioning their world view. They are reluctant to talk about this openly, and have difficulty in relating it to orthodox religious talk which seems stereotyped and impersonal. There is a chasm between the pupils' experiences and questions about commitment, and the way in which religions are normally expressed and taught. The religious education teacher has to bridge this chasm before he is in business. To make a bridge he has to do two things: firstly, to help his pupils appreciate that the experience of living raises questions of truth and meaning and life-styles that no sensitive and alert person can avoid, and that religions and non-theistic life stances are concerned with dealing with those questions; secondly, to assist the pupils to understand the language that religions use in discussing those questions, a language that is not the straightforward descriptive talk that is used by the sciences, but a language of myth, story, parable and allegory.[4] Religious education in the past has tended to neglect this spade-work, and gone directly to teaching about religious tenets and ceremonies, which may be the reason why it has often seemed to pupils to be talking about things that don't directly matter in a language that doesn't make sense.

The Teacher's Commitments

The teacher of religious education will probably have a religious commitment; he certainly ought to have a commitment to education. Those who deal with the subject need to bear in mind how their religious commitment affects the manner in which they handle the diverse materials in the syllabus, and how it can come into conflict with their educational obligations.

Educationally the obligations of a teacher of religious education are no different from those of his colleagues. It is expected that all pedagogues will be committed to

(a) the welfare of the pupils;
(b) the pupils' growth as intellectual beings;
(c) the pupils' integration into their culture and their society;
(d) the imparting to the pupils skills of discovering, knowing, and evaluating;
(e) the fostering of the pupils' liberal thought and rationality;
(g) their own academic study;
(h) the need for that study as an essential part of a full education.

It is usually the case that, in addition to these educational commitments, the religious education teacher has certain religious beliefs which impinge upon his work. Many have chosen to teach the subject because they have had some contact with, or experience of, religion which has aroused their interest. Formerly the majority of them were probably inspired by evangelizing zeal, with a desire to share with pupils what they had enjoyed and to transmit insights which had been important to them. No one wondered at this, but with the coming of the 'new' religious education, with its study of many world faiths and its phobias about indoctrination and about lack of respect for pupils' autonomy, there has been a tendency to think evangelizing zeal not only unnecessary, but a distinct handicap. Certainly an attachment to one point of view, held in the hard way described above, with the corresponding assumption that all other faiths are mistaken and possibly pernicious, will not help the teacher to present fairly and with understanding the other beliefs which the syllabus may prescribe for study, nor make it easy for him to understand sympathetically a pluralist culture and the attitudes and needs of the pupils within that culture.

Nevertheless, it is usually expected that those who undertake to teach about religion in schools should be connected, or have been connected in the past, with some form of religion. It would be thought peculiar if a music teacher had never listened to or made music, or if a games teacher had never played games. Geography teachers are expected to have travelled and seen something of the lands they describe, and modern language teachers are thought the better for having lived in the countries whose languages they teach. Similarly, the religious education teacher is expected to have had vital experiential contact with some of what he teaches about, and to be able to extend to the remainder of his lesson content the insight that that contact has given him. Nor is this an unreasonable demand, since an understanding of religion involves not only a knowledge of its tenets, ceremonies and moral practices but also an insight into what it feels like to the adherents to believe and practise in that way. If, then, understanding a religion does require experience of it at some time, even if one reviews that experience objectively and critically afterwards, then genuine religious commitment at some time is a prerequisite for the religious education teacher.

This puts that teacher in a difficult position. Educational theorists and the public generally are asking two things of him which it is not all that easy to reconcile. On the one hand, he has to be acquainted with a religion, and know the meaning of faith and the feeling of belonging to a religious body; on the other hand he has to teach with an openness which too firm an attachment to religion can make difficult. Because of this the religious education teacher is exposed to the possibility of tension between his religious and his educational commitments. The former lead him to think that certain things are true, certain actions are good, certain beliefs are genuine, and that other beliefs and actions are at least inferior if not misguided; the latter require that he study all beliefs objectively with the possibility that the beliefs with which he agrees (and which matter to him deeply) might be false, and that those with which he disagrees might be true. He has, as far as he can, to present them all impartially and make them all equally available to the pupils for acceptance or rejection. The self-abnegation and nervous tension that result can be considerable, and more self-restraint is required than in most other school subjects if a free and workable relationship is to be maintained between teacher and learners. There must be tension when a pupil rejects, perhaps in an adolescent, scornful and aggressive way, the cherished beliefs of the teacher, or when he enthusiastically, and equally aggressively, champions a way of life that the teacher thinks to be wrong or harmful. In such a situation the teacher has to find a way of maintaining friendly relationships and preserving a respect for pupil autonomy without incurring a sense of disloyalty to his own convictions.

The practical problems faced by a religiously committed teacher are:

(a) how to teach about his own religion without over-presenting it;

(b) how to deal with other faiths and ideologies without under-selling them;

(c) how to understand and relate to pupils who disapprove of his beliefs and express others, so that he doesn't fall into the trap of relating only to those who share his views and appearing to have favourites.

One way of solving these problems is for the teacher to modify his religious commitments. It could be argued that they are inappropriate in a classroom situation, and that one who is indifferent to all religious beliefs is most likely to teach about religions fairly. That could well lead to a cynical and unenthusiastic study. A stronger case can be made for a genuine agnosticism on the teacher's part, because a searching agnosticism allows respect for all beliefs and admits the possibility that any of them could lead to truth.[5] Moreover, an agnostic teacher will be able to join the pupils in their searching and this will make the study a co-operative enquiry. It is questionable, however, whether religious convictions can be so abandoned or moderated to an agnosticism. The teacher is stuck with his convictions, and it may be better for him to be frank about them, to hold them firmly and sincerely, and to tell his pupils what they are, so that allowances can be made for the way they colour his presentation and his judgments. A confident belief can be more tolerant and objective than a half-faith, a doubted and fearing faith, which has to protect itself by refusing to contemplate the possibility of error or of alternative truth, and which has to be rigidly advocated and oversold, to allay the unadmitted doubts of the teacher as much as convince the pupil.

This confident but unaggressive sort of belief entails a further commitment which has not so far been mentioned, namely a commitment to the belief that genuine study and a critical search for understanding will lead to truth. Then there is no need to put up barriers to honest enquiry. One's own religion can be subjected to the same objective scrutiny as the others, because one is confident that it can stand up to critical study and to unreserved comparison, because its truth will be apparent. Perhaps next to a searching agnosticism, a deep faith and trust in one's religion, and this conviction that the 'truth will out', is the best equipment for a religious education teacher.

It is possible that some forms of religion permit this open enquiry more than others. Those with a strong belief in a revealed truth enshrined in an inspired sacred literature (such as Jehovah's Witnesses and most orthodox Muslims) find it difficult, and consequently tend to think of religious education, not as a critical study of religions, but as transmitting their beliefs and culture to their young. Religions with a developed belief in human free-will find it easier. Certain types of Christians have recently claimed that their beliefs have the respect for man's freedom and for liberal search that enables their adherents to teach religious education with a high degree of detached unaggression. This is a newish claim (Torquemada, Calvin and even Wesley might have found it difficult to accept) but it may be true none the less.

If a teacher becomes conscious that his religious commitments are conflicting with his educational obligations, the latter should determine what he does in the classroom. There his purpose is to lead pupils to study religions with the object of understanding them. He is not, as a teacher, concerned with conversion to any one of them. That is the work of religious bodies. Outside school, the teacher, as a member of a religious body, may be a preacher, an active evangelist, or train youth in the faith by running a church club or Sunday school. Those he speaks to in such contexts are able to remove themselves if they find his influence unacceptable. Pupils in school cannot remove themselves, and their autonomy of belief ought to be respected. In teaching them about religion the teacher has to recognise the limits that his role as a teacher imposes. He must confine himself to what is educationally proper, as he usually does with other things, such as promoting his political views or indulging a delighted capacity for telling suggestive stories. There is a proper self-discipline for a teacher, and this extends to his beliefs as well as to other habits and parts of his personality. Should his religious beliefs, which tend by their very nature to be imperative, make this impossible, he ought to consider how far they are impairing his educational efficiency, and whether he ought to continue teaching the subject.

NOTES

1   M. Paffard (1973).
2   E. Robinson (1977).
3   Paffard, *op. cit.*, p. 145.
4   The problem of religious language is discussed more fully in Chapter Six, below.
5   The position of the agnostic teacher is examined in E. Cox (1977).

5 The Problem of Dealing with Sacred Literature

In the older Agreed Syllabuses Bible Study took a disproportionate space, and indeed often seemed to constitute the whole of the content. The reasons for this were both practical and historical. Practically, the Bible was a book readily available for reading at a time when education was more literary-based than now, and when there were few alternative texts for the subject. Historically, there were two influences at work. Firstly, the religion with which the syllabuses were almost exclusively concerned was Protestant Christianity which, since its origin at the Reformation, had possessed a strong Biblical element. Having rejected the authority of a Church, the Protestants found it necessary to replace it by some other ground of appeal, and the Bible provided that new authority. For them religion became closely linked with knowledge of and obedience to the Bible text. Secondly, as a result of the denominational suspicions up to the First World War, religious education in Britain was confined almost entirely to Biblical study. The Cowper-Temple clause forbade the teaching of any formularies distinctive of a denomination in schools without church affiliations but all denominations could agree that the Bible was the source-book of Christianity, and so by confining the subject to a study of it, often 'without note or comment', controversy was avoided. This link of religious education with Bible study dies hard. Pupils are still inclined to ask 'What has this to do with religion?' if the lesson does not include a Biblical reference, and it is illuminating that the Northamptonshire Agreed Syllabus of 1980 includes, in its chapter on Music and Religion, not only sections on how music is used in religions to express feelings, and on bells and bell-ringing, but also a section on 'musical instruments of the Bible'.

None the less, for a number of reasons the study of sacred

literature now takes less time in the classroom and less space in the more recent syllabuses. The implicit religion approach and the extension of the curriculum to include non-Christian religions and life-stances mean that other things have had to be accorded time that was formerly given to Bible study. Sacred writings are not as prominent in those religions as the Bible is in Protestant Christianity, with the possible exceptions of the Torah in Judaism and the Qur'ān in Islam. In addition, the scriptures of those religions are not so readily available or so well known to many of the teachers as is the Bible. They have less influential contact with British general culture. What is more, the Bible has come to take a less noticeable place in British life and is not so well known, even to Christians. The phenomenological approach to religious education has drawn attention to the fact that response to sacred literature is only one part of religious practice. Ninian Smart's description of religion as having six dimensions (the doctrinal, the mythical, the ethical, the ritual, the experiential and the social), set out in his *Secular Education and the Logic of Religion*,[1] has been particularly influential in showing teachers that an adequate study of a religion involves much more than reading its sacred books.

Nevertheless, study of sacred scriptures has its place in religious education. They play an integral part in religions and some idea of their origins, their relationship to the doctrines, their contribution to the moral code, their use in worship, and of how they are understood and valued by believers, is needed for a satisfactory knowledge of religion.

In the case of the Christian Bible, there may be a further reason for including it. Throughout the years, the Bible has contributed a great deal to European culture, influencing literature, the texts of major musical works, the judicial system and the general trends of morality. This influence may be diminishing and the sacred books of other religions may come in time to make similar contributions, but for the moment, knowledge of the Bible is needed for insight into much of Milton and Shakespeare, a Beethoven Mass, certain Mendelssohn and Elgar oratorios, not to mention the novels of Thomas Hardy and more modern works such as *Belshazzar's Feast*, *Godspell* and *Jesus Christ Superstar*. There is justification for studying the Bible apart from its religious significance.

The nature of sacred books, and the manner in which they function within the circle of believers, makes them a difficult school study. They raise problems both of lesson presentation and of pupil understanding, problems which worry all teachers who do not approach them from a fundamentalist point of view. In using them in the religious education lesson five considerations have to be borne in mind.

(a) The historical remove

One thing that the sacred books of all religions have in common is that they are old. They come from a time when customs, language, ways of thought, methods of earning a living and of finding recreation were very different from those used in the mobile, industrialized, televised, computer-controlled, group-organised world in which present-day schoolchildren live. Furthermore, from a British point of view, they all come from countries far away – the nearest being the Middle East. They tell of a way of life remote in time and space, which has to be understood if the writings are to be seen to have meaning. This requires considerable background knowledge of the culture involved and a well-developed historical imagination which children, especially the younger ones, may not yet have acquired. Without it, there is the possibility that pupils will either regard scriptures as too far from their experience to be intelligible or worth learning about, or that they will project their experience onto scriptural characters (for instance, they might imagine the Israelites under Moses and the Egyptians under Pharaoh fighting with planes and tanks, or think that Mary and Joseph in Bethlehem tried to put up at the 'White Horse' or the 'King's Head') so that they get a distorted view. Trying to overcome this difficulty, teachers can take up most of their lesson time with background details, descriptions of life and customs and food and dress and architecture (not forgetting those musical instruments) in Palestine or Persia or India, with the result that they seem to be teaching about historical cultures and not about the writings at all.

(b) The intellectual and linguistic remove

Another gulf to be bridged is that between the assumptions and language of the scriptural writers and those in common currency today. The writers of the Qur'ān, the Bhagavad-Gītā, the Pāli Pitakas, and the various books of the Old and New Testaments, had differing world views, none of which is identical with that employed in our culture, influenced as it is by the physical sciences. Their assumptions about what is real were not so closely tied to empiricism so that they were free to express their conception of the world and its significance in more imaginative ways than would be acceptable to modern taste. Moreover, they were frequently concerned with the significance of the created world and the things that happen in it rather than in merely describing what they saw. They were writing to express their beliefs, and those beliefs affected how they wrote of history and what they assumed to be true and possible. They were, in addition, writing in ages when ideas were incorporated in stories and imaginative sayings (witness Homer, Aesop, Ovid and others) and in particular examples rather than in abstract, generalised terms. This affects the form of their writing and their language (in the sense of how they communicate rather than in their grammar and their syntax). In lessons about scriptures, therefore, one comes up against the difficulty of religious language, which is discussed more fully in Chapter 6.

(c) The liturgical and devotional function of sacred writings

Though sacred writings contain doctrines and are sometimes, as in the case of the Epistle to the Ephesians, systematic expositions of theological ideas, they are not used only as manuals of doctrine. In addition to being regarded as a record of a religion's teaching in its formative years and as a court of appeal in cases of doctrinal dispute, they are used in Christianity, Islam and Judaism in a formal, liturgical way, and in all religions as an aid to individual devotions. They are read ceremoniously in worship and given special respect by the manner in which they are brought to the reader, or by the use of a formula before or after the reading. This gives them an extrinsic significance for the believer present at worship. They acquire associations. Other things that are said and done in the worship, its ideas and aspirations, are psychologically attached to them, to be evoked when they are later read or heard. So when a believer reads, or hears read, one of the scriptures of his faith, it will have overtones and bring thoughts which are not necessarily directly related to the passage.

> Given certain conditions, religious feelings of real value may be evoked by such a use of the Scriptures even without clear understanding . . . They owe their effect not in the first place to their intelligible meaning, but to the 'aura' of sacred association surrounding them.[2]

This 'aura of sacred association' is at work in the 'devotional' reading of sacred books and in meditation based upon them. When a believer alone, or in company with a small group of similar experience and belief, reads his scriptures in order to receive 'edification' or spiritual reassurance, the thoughts that come to his mind after reading may not arise specifically from the text. They are, none the less, evoked by the scripture in a way that they would not be evoked if another type of literature was being used. They occur because of the respect that the reader has for the writing before him and because of the religious associations that it has acquired by its previous ceremonial and devotional use.

There is another way in which belief affects the reading of scriptures so that they are understood in a peculiar way. The believer projects his belief into what he is reading so that it says something to him that a non-believer would not recognise. Perhaps this is best explained by a specific example. In the Christian scriptures there is a story of Jesus as a boy of twelve being found among the Temple teachers asking them questions,[3] which Christians not infrequently interpret and relate as a proof of Jesus' omniscience. Their belief that Jesus is the son of an omniscient God causes them also to believe that he himself must have been omniscient, so that, even as a boy of twelve, he would know far more than the Temple teachers, the greatest scholars in Palestine at the time. They consequently understand the story as telling that Jesus was submitting those scholars to an interrogation which they were finding beyond their capacity to answer. The Bible text, however, says that Jesus was 'sitting among the doctors, both hearing them and asking them questions' and that they 'were amazed at his understanding and his answers'. To a non-Christian reader it would seem an example of an intelligent youth asking questions in order to learn, and showing acumen both by the relevance of the questions and by his sensible reaction to the answers. Seen in that light, it is a story about Jesus' intelligence, not about his omniscience. Similar projections of belief are liable to occur whenever scriptures are being read by one who holds the faith to which they belong.

That scriptures are understood by religious men and women in these associative and belief-influenced ways has two implications for the classroom. The first is that a sacred text will have different meaning for pupils belonging to the religion that regards it as sacred from what it will for the others. The former will bring to it a respect and a wealth of associated ideas. They will see meanings and significances in it which are extrinsic to the words, and which will not be apparent to their fellows. This difference of response quickly becomes obvious if one is studying the New Testament with a class that contains Christians, Jews and atheists. It is not suggested that the reaction of believers is either right or wrong, but that the teacher has to recognise the diverse response that can arise and arrange his strategy so that all can feel that they have learned something from the study, and not be given the impression that they are over-imaginative because they see rather more or myopic because they see rather less.

The second implication is that the teacher must beware of how these associated and extrinsic ideas that attach themselves to the text can colour his presentation when he is dealing with the scriptures of his own religion, for he may then be confining his teaching to those who share his beliefs. Such breakdown of communication has often occurred in the past when religious education was mainly thought of as teaching the Bible to the young of a Christian culture.

It is perhaps the mistake of syllabus makers and many religious education teachers to assume that all pupils respond to Bible study as though they were convinced church-goers.[4]

(d) The idea of inspiration

The reason why religions set certain books apart and call them 'scriptures' is because they are thought to be inspired. The truth of them is guaranteed in a way that does not apply to other literature. Inspiration can vary from a belief that the very words themselves are God-given, with the writers being mechanical transcribers of what is set down and making no contribution to it with their minds, to a more generalised acceptance that the ideas are inerrant even though the forms in which they are expressed are liable to accident and human error. The point that teachers have to take into account is that this is a belief. There is nothing in any scriptures themselves that make it plainly apparent to any reader who picks them up that they are such infallible statements. They are taken to be such by the believer because he has first made an act of faith that his God can so inspire writings and that the text before him is an example of that inspiration. Even when a scripture makes a claim such as that made in the second Epistle to Timothy in the New Testament that 'all scripture is given by inspiration of

God',[5] although it may reinforce the belief of those who already think that way, it will not convince the sceptic who will feel free to think that it is a circular argument to affirm that a writing is inspired because it makes such a claim for itself.

Therefore, although inspiration may be assumed or taken for granted when a sacred book is being studied within its own faith – in a Church meeting, a synagogue, or a Sunday School – it has to remain an open matter in the schools of a secular society. The teacher cannot say, 'This is inspired, we don't question it.' Instead, the scripture has to undergo the same critical scrutiny that is applied to all other literature. Yet belief in inspiration will be influencing how the believing pupil reacts to the lesson and how the believing teacher presents it. This is a further example of the need of a believing teacher to beware of allowing his faith to colour overmuch his handling of the lesson material.

(e) The idea of revealed knowledge

Closely connected with the notion of inspiration, and indeed flowing from it, is the idea of 'revealed knowledge'. Because he accepts their inspiration, the religious believer thinks that through the scriptures his God has shown him certain knowledge about the nature of that God, about reality and about moral living. This 'revealed knowledge' has certain characteristics. It is of a sort that men could not come upon it by any other way, or could not obtain it for a very long time. It therefore enables the human race to know things, or to know them more quickly, that would otherwise be long concealed from it. Moreover, this 'knowledge' differs from discovered knowledge in that it cannot be verified by the processes we normally use to check up on what we claim to know. It has to be accepted by that same act of faith that produces acceptance of the inspiration of scripture.

In a pluralist society there is bound to be a mixed reaction to revealed 'knowledge'. The religious man is confident of the truth that he believes to be available in his scriptures and is prepared to allow it to influence his life and to act upon it. To others this may seem like a superstition. The 'truth' a Christian finds in the Bible may not necessarily look like a 'truth' to a Humanist; the 'knowledge' that a Muslim claims is made plain in the Qur'ān may not seem to a Buddhist to have the status of knowledge. The situation, however, is not entirely clear-cut. There are common elements in the scriptures of many religions which allow a measure of agreement between religious people, even if that agreement does not extend to the Humanist, the materialist and the sceptic. Furthermore, revealed 'knowledge' can be verified to some extent by experience. If a person makes an act of faith that a certain piece of information is revealed in scriptures, acts in the light of it, and finds that, as a result, his life is meaningful, orderly and satisfying, he may think that his faith is justified and that scripture has brought him genuine knowledge. The sceptic may concede that the knowledge is genuine but not accept a religious explanation of its origin, thinking that theories of inspiration and revelation are metaphorical ways of describing what, in fact, has been discovered by chance or trial and error. This is a common attitude in England, where many will agree with the wisdom of the Ten Commandments or the Sermon on the Mount, while having strong doubts as to whether the Decalogue was revealed supernaturally to Moses or as to whether Jesus was divine. The effect of this on the teaching situation is that the pragmatic argument that revealed knowledge seems to work in practice and, therefore, the revelation is genuine, cannot be used in the classroom as it can in religious apology and homily, because it will not carry conviction to those who have not already accepted the validity of revelation.

The charge that religious education is indoctrinatory arises largely from the way in which this revealed 'knowledge' is used in the teaching. If the teacher gives the impression that it is unquestionably true and universally agreed there is some justification for that charge, since he is conditioning the pupils to accept uncritically the beliefs of a particular religious body. It is also a self-defeating practice pedagogically, for pupils are aware too of the pluralistic nature of society and will recognise that he is elevating the beliefs of a section of society to the status of facts. They may not challenge the teaching in so many words; instead, they are inclined to withdraw their attention and to hold both the subject and the teacher in a thinly veiled scorn. The part played in religion by the idea of revealed knowledge is, however, so centrally important that it has to be included in any serious study. It cannot be avoided but it needs to be handled sensitively, critically, and with an understanding of its nature.

The Educational Approach to Sacred Literature

Bearing in mind the considerations set out above, the teacher will realise that there are problems to be solved if lessons about sacred literature are not to be mystifying, misleading and indoctrinatory.

The difficulties that arise from the historical remoteness and the thought-forms and language of the material (see (a) and (b) above) are unlikely to be overcome except with pupils who have matured sufficiently to have acquired an historical sense and an awareness of the complexity of language and an appreciation of how metaphorical, allegorical and mythological speech are, in their own way, as valid a means of conveying appropriate truths as are factual statements. This demands a high degree of intellectual development that is likely to be found only in the higher classes. For that reason it has been argued that the study of sacred literature should not be undertaken in the primary school. Yet younger children are going to encounter those stories from scriptures that are part of the culture in which they live. For instance, it is inconceivable that children in a region influenced by Christianity should not come across stories of Noah's Ark and of the nativity of Jesus, and the same probably holds in other religious cultures. What is more, young children find these tales intriguing, as tales, and do not often worry about whether or not they have deeper significance. They understand the stories in their own way, and it is only later, in adolescence, that the historical and linguistic removes cause difficulties. If, at that stage, the stories are not to be rejected as childish entertainments, but recognised as being taken seriously by religious people and having significance for them, more teaching needs to be done than is often allowed for about the nature of the writings, the thought-forms which were natural to their writers, and the literary forms and languages in which they expressed their ideas. Teaching and discussion about this at the appropriate time (possibly about the ages of twelve to fifteen) might prevent ignorant revulsion to further study.

The problems raised by associative and belief-influenced interpretations of scriptures and by theories of inspiration and revelation (see (c), (d), and (e) above) become less intractable if we set the study of scriptures in the context of what religious education in general is trying to achieve. If the purpose of the subject is to promote an understanding of religions and of how they influence values and actions, rather than to convert to any one of them, then sacred books will be studied, not with the object of presenting them as either true or false, but in order to teach how they are used and understood by believers. This involves imparting an idea of how religions use their scriptures in worship, of how this affects the understanding of scriptures by those who experience them so used, and of how religious people read their sacred texts devotionally and interpret them in the light of their belief, and of how all this contributes to their outlook and reinforces their confidence in their faith. The purpose of the teacher, in the first place, is to give information about the functioning of sacred writings in religious systems. Pupils will, of course, be assessing what they learn, and deciding whether they agree or disagree with such use of scriptures, and those who belong to the religion being studied will agree more readily than the others. It is to be hoped that believers will learn to appreciate more deeply the nature of their scriptures and of the influence and functioning of sacred writings in their own religion; they may also acquire increased sympathy with how those in other religions use and respond to sacred texts. Hardline non-believers will probably still find the whole business alien to their experience, but they may learn a tolerance towards the manner in which many people's lives and judgments are influenced by sacred literature, and even an understanding of it.

Granted such an approach to the teaching, revealed 'truths' or revealed 'knowledge' causes less contention, since the pupil is not faced with the stark choice of accepting it as true or of rejecting it as the delusions of a set of cranks. Indeed, the question of its truth or falsehood, its acceptability or unacceptability, is not raised in the first instance, although it has eventually to be faced. Pupils will inevitably be making up their minds how far they agree with what they are studying, but if this is delayed they will be deciding informedly and not from instantaneous gut reaction or prejudice.

In dealing with scriptures, teachers can attempt the following activities without infringing pupils' intellectual freedom:

(a)   They can teach that there are those who hold certain books as sacred and as bringing them information which they regard as true; that is, teach about the *belief* in inspiration and its expression in scriptures.

(b)   They can impart information of what different religions claim is revealed in their sacred books. This is mere description of what men and women do, in fact, believe wihout the implication that members of the class should believe it too.

(c) They can show how religious people use their scriptures in worship and meditation, and the effect that this has on them.

(d) In the higher forms, it may be possible for them to initiate discussion of how far these claimed revelations are borne out by human experience, and of how far they can consequently be regarded as probably true or false. Occasionally, there may be the possibility of going even further and discussing the phenomenon of inspiration and considering what leads men to think they have intuited truth directly, and the means they employ to write about that experience.

It will be obvious that to teach about sacred literature in this way demands a particular attitude on the part of the teacher and one which a deep and emotional attachment to any one set of scriptures will make difficult. It requires an objectivity which can look on the scriptures of other faiths with sympathy and on the scriptures of his own faith, if he has one, with detachment. This is not to advocate insincerity, and if, in discussion, the teacher is questioned about his own attitude to scriptures, he should answer frankly since his beliefs are part of the evidence which pupils have to consider of how sacred writings are understood by believers. This is a further example of how a teacher must recognise the potential tension between his religious commitment and his function as a teacher and exercise a self-discipline in order to be able to approach the study of scriptures with both sympathy and detachment. For, in a sceptical age, with its plurality of religious beliefs, all of which are questioned by someone, any other method of dealing with sacred literature in schools can hardly be justified on educational grounds.

NOTES

1　N. Smart (1968).
2　C. H. Dodd (1938, p.4).
3　Luke 2, 41-47.
4　E. Cox, 'The Bible in religious education' in N. Smart and D. Horder (eds) (1975, p.236).
5　II Timothy 3, 16.

6 The Problem of Religious Language

Mention has already been made (page 53 above) of the chasm that the teacher has to bridge between pupils' experience and the way in which religion is usually expressed and taught within a faith system. Much that goes on in the religious education lesson seems artificial and irrelevant to pupils, not because they are unconcerned with the issues being raised, but because of the language and thought forms with which those issues are being discussed. There is an example in the Bullock Report, *A Language for Life*,[1] of the disjunction that can occur when a teacher and a pupil are using different types of language. When asked to describe the making of a wormery, a thirteen-year-old wrote in personal terms of his experience of making such an object, and, notwithstanding that he wrote adequately from that point of view, had his work adjudged 'not very good' because the teacher was thinking in terms of an impersonal objective, practical statement in the style of a manual of instruction. Similar misunderstanding can occur in religious education when teacher and pupil are playing different language games.

The misunderstanding arises from the confusion of what Harold Rosen has called *transactional* language (which 'demands accurate and scientific reference to what is known about reality') and *expressive* language,[2] and from the disposition of the twentieth century secular and technological culture to look on religious talk as almost wholly transactional. It would, however, be equally misleading to go to the other extreme and think that religious talk is entirely expressive, because religion uses both types of converse. When dealing with the history of a religion, with the dates and place of origin of its founder, and with observed details of how the worshippers behave and so on, the teacher is using transactional language similar to that of the historian or sociologist and can expect to be plainly understood by the class. But religious talk includes feelings and values and intimations (rather than demonstrable, graspable knowledge) about reality, and this demands expressive and figurative language, stories and poems and parables, which, if taken literally, or thought about literal-mindedly, either fail to communicate or lead to absurdities.

Misunderstanding of religious language occurs in the classroom, and elsewhere for that matter, at different levels. Firstly, there are problems of technical terms and symbols; secondly, there are problems resulting from the tendency of a culture greatly influenced by the physical sciences to devalue expressive or figurative statements; thirdly, there are difficulties that arise from the interlinking of experiential and value statements with statements of reality; and fourthly, there are confusions about the use of myths at the present development of human thinking.

Technical Terms and Symbols

All forms of understanding evolve their own terminology and symbology and religion is no exception. Each religion has its own set of technical terms which have been worked out by its scholars and thinkers and which they use with precise meaning – terms such as salvation, karma, Messiah, nirvana, sin and forgiveness, and so on. Learning about them, and learning to use them, is unquestionably part of religious education, but there are two obstructions to it. The first is that because religion has been interwoven with general culture those technical terms are often used in everyday conversation in a more generalised sense. Consequently they do not convey the precise meanings of a scientific term (e.g. appendicitis, or isometric) which evokes a similar and exact understanding every time it is used. They have the same disadvantage as, for instance, the word 'tolerance', which has a precise meaning when used by the engineer and a more diffuse one when applied to human relationships. To take one example, the word 'sin' is popularly bandied about to apply to all grades of crimes and peccadilloes, whereas theologically it should refer only to an action made in defiance of the known will of a God.[3] When, therefore, technical religious terms are used, without definition, in the religious education lesson, they transmit a confused and degraded impression and can seem to the learners to be connotating something far less important than intended. The religion under discussion is thereby trivialised.

The other difficulty with such terms is that the teacher, having studied the subject widely, uses these terms freely, and the pupils do the same, without relating them to their own experience unless specifically helped to do so. This leads to verbalism, to making the right religious noises, rather than to expressing understanding, and eventually can produce the attitude that religious talk is a wordiness to which it is impossible to attach genuine meaning. Religious education is not alone in this, for as Rosen has written, the blind, uncomprehending use of scholarly language is found across the curriculum.

> The language in the text-book, on the blackboard, and in the mouth of the teacher can be aped relatively easily but this does not make it available for considered, appropriate, individual use.[4]

The practical implication of this is that conscious attention has to be given in the classroom to the technical language of religion. The words need to be explained and used in their exact sense in lessons so that secondary school pupils come to recognise that there is a language that will allow theological issues to be examined with precision and that religion need not be discussed in the confused and turbulent manner of the devotional tract or the ill-considered sermon.

Besides being mediated in technical terms religious ideas are frequently clothed in symbolic form. Religious talk is rich in symbols, which are of two kinds, one of which needs more complex handling in teaching than the other. There are symbols, which might perhaps be called archetypal, which seem to belong deep in the human psyche and which are used over the spectrum of belief systems. These are formed by the figurative use of terms such as light and darkness, ascent and descent, night and day, washing or cleansing, sonship, and so on. Provided they are recognised as symbols, and not confused with the factual use of the terms in other contexts, these are not particularly liable to misunderstanding and pupils respond to them and can be encouraged to use them and to express them in drawings, imaginative writings, drama and movement. They do this with greater facility if they have been examining symbolic expression in other fields, and there is scope here for collaboration between the religious education teacher and his colleagues who teach art, literature, music and drama. The sciences might also be involved, since they too have their symbols.

More difficult are the symbols that are peculiar to a specific religion, which have been fashioned by the history and experience of that faith, and which can be understood fully only in relation to their origins and the events and pressures that have produced them. These symbols may centre round an object, such as the cross in the case of Christianity; or an idea, as in the wheel of life in eastern religions; or in an action, as in the hadj in Islam; or in a ceremony such as Passover or Hanukkah in Judaism. These have a deep significance for the religion that uses them, which they do not have for others. They do not communicate across the faith boundaries. The symbol of the cross has a richness of association for the Christian which it does not have for the Muslim; the symbol of Passover means much to the Jew but little to the Hindu. There is, as a result, a breakdown of communication if a teacher uses a symbol to carry the associations that it has in its own religious context to pupils who have not lived in that context. What religious education can do, however, is to teach how these symbols are used in their proper setting and what they mean to those who use them. This involves explaining their origins. It is not possible to grasp what Passover means to the Jews without knowing something of the history of their race and the story of the Exodus, nor is it possible to appreciate why Christians use the symbol of the cross without knowing the story of the crucifixion and how the Christians came to relate it to older Hebrew theories of sacrifice and used it to explain to themselves their feelings about Jesus. A comparative study of these culturally conditioned symbols, of their emergence and their use within a faith setting to express religious insights and aspirations, could form an enlightening element in the religious education syllabus.

The Influence of Scientific Thinking on the Understanding of Religion

There is a more ultimate difficulty about religious language at present than that caused by misunderstanding of its words and symbols. There is the question of what exactly that language is trying to say through its vocabulary and its symbols, a question that has become particularly acute in the twentieth century because of the influence on thinking of the success of the 'scientific method'.

The thought of mediaeval Christendom was mainly otherwordly. Life was seen as a probation, carried on in a temporary and unsatisfactory world which men tended to ignore (if they could not exploit it) and to judge in terms of another spiritual world to which they believed they were going. Even power-grasping politicians in the moment of truth before they were beheaded made speeches acknowledging that other world as the true one and the source of values. But the Renaissance, by recovering a good deal of classical humanism, called attention to the physical world and its beauties and possibilities. Men began to look at the world around them, to examine it, and, more significantly, to measure it and note its uniformities. That investigation was found to yield greater results if it was conducted impersonally and without value judgments or presuppositions as to the nature or origin of matter, and so the scientific spirit was born.

The uniformities and consistencies discovered in the behaviour of matter were codified into 'scientific laws' and these enabled men to understand physical phenomena which previously had seemed arbitrary and magical, and, more important, to predict accurately how matter could be expected to behave under given conditions. It was but a small step to apply the new knowledge in practice. Inventors followed the scientific investigators to put their knowledge to use by making the uniformities of nature work for them in the form of machines, medicines, fertilisers and the like. The result was the Industrial Revolution in those areas where power was readily available. The full impact of the process and its capability of transforming the environment and the quality of human life has been felt only in the last fifty or sixty years when automobiles, aviation, radio communication, electronic calculation, new medical techniques, nuclear fission, space travel, and the application of vast machines to the rapid modification of the environment have radically changed the quality of life within the span of one man's memory.

The practical success of the scientific method has given it a prestige and makes it seem to reveal a superior kind of truth. Some even go so far as to claim that it is the only road to truth, and most of us feel more secure when thinking in terms of the testable and the demonstrable with which science and technology deals than when we are concerned with more debatable matters of aesthetic preference and belief. The effect on ways of thinking about what is ultimately real is fourfold.

(a)   It has produced a tendency to make a sharp distinction between knowledge that is susceptible to testing in the scientific manner and that which is not capable of being so verified.

(b) It has encouraged the feeling that physical demonstrability is the only test of truth.

(c) Following from this there is a degrading of other types of experience. Moral judgments, artistic tastes and religious beliefs cannot be subjected to the same compelling public verification as scientific fact – the only numerical process that can be applied to them is the sociological counting of heads of those who hold a particular opinion, taste or belief – so they seem less true, in the way that scientific facts seem true, and we feel cautious, and perhaps incapable, of discriminating between them. Morals, tastes and religions become hobbies, similar to coarse fishing or chess playing, pleasant for those who indulge in them, but having no claim on general attention and yielding no knowledge of the nature of reality.

(d) This leads to the devaluing of personality. If one suspects the validity of personal opinions, and insists that only those investigations that have completely eliminated the personal element can lead to a knowledge of the truth, then human beings and human personalities do not seem very important. There is an inclination to regard a human being as another chunk of matter subject to mechanical causation motivated, not by choice, but by the movement of electrical currents in the brain, whose behaviour is decided by factors beyond mortal control and which could be predicted and modified if only we knew enough about those factors. This discounting of human choices and of the interplay of personality in society considerably modifies our approach to philosophy and religion.

In philosophy this outlook produced the Logical Positivist philosophy which, having begun in Vienna, was brought to this country by A. J. Ayer and systematically set out in his *Language, Truth and Logic*.[5] At its most extreme it was the philosophy of the natural sciences, insisting through its Verification Principle that only those statements that can be tested by sense reference have any meaning. All other statements, such as 'I love Lucy', 'The Mona Lisa is beautiful', or 'I believe in God', are 'non-sense' and consequently meaningless. Religion fares badly when this type of reasoning is applied to it. Many of its statements, such as 'There is a God', 'Allah is merciful', 'Jesus saves', and so on cannot be subjected to the sort of testing that the verification principle demands, or result in absurdity when such a test is applied. Religious talk is 'non-sense',[6] it is not telling us anything about the world as it is, and if it is talking about something else then our predilection for sense testing makes it appear dubious, inferior and possibly meaningless.

The philosophers have recently considerably modified their position but it takes time for the latest thoughts of leading philosophers to percolate through to the man in the street and the sixth-former in the library, and the older ideas are still influential, particularly when applied to religion. Moreover, many who would not understand a closely reasoned philosophical argument are prepared to accept that religion has been proved meaningless because it resolves their own less-deeply examined doubts about whether religion has any part in a technologically controlled culture.

Put into its simplest form, the difficulty about religion is this. If scientific language, with its insistence on sensible verification to establish meaning, is the reliable way to talk about what is real, and religion claims to talk about what is real, then it ought to be able to express its insights in scientific language. Religious language is either scientific language or it is not; if it is not then it is meaningless; and if it is, then its statements have to stand up to comparison with scientific statements. But frequently they do not stand up to that comparison and so a rational man has to choose between them. If they are talking the same language and making contradictory assertions, one cannot have both. One or the other is wrong. That is the end of religious talk unless it can be shown that it is talking about something else that is worth talking about.

The confusion of religious language with scientific language is illustrated by the controversy which so often comes up in the classroom over the theory of evolution and the creation story in Genesis. If Genesis is giving a factual account of the origin of the universe (that is, if it is a scientific statement) then it does not square with evolutionary theory and one has to decide which has got nearer to the truth. But if Genesis is talking another kind of language, and providing not a factual account of the origin of the universe but an imaginative story of the belief which some hold of the relationship between God and creation, then both views may be held and the conflict disappears.

It is the same confusion that gives point to Flew's use of John Wisdom's parable about the explorers in the jungle clearing to expose the difficulty of religious language.[7] One explorer reacts to the sight of the clearing by saying, 'Some gardener must tend this plot.' The other disagrees and sets up all sorts of mechanical devices to detect the gardener, without positive result, and forces his companion to make so many qualifications to his original statement that it is emptied of meaning. The second explorer has taken the original statement to be a factual one. He assumes that his companion uses the word 'gardener' to refer to a finite individual, with gardening boots and an apron, who comes with tools and seeds to rearrange the vegetation. But the first explorer knew quite well that no such a gardener existed in a primitive and unexplored jungle. Even if he was referring to a God he would not intend some aproned gardener writ large, such as could be detected by electrical and mechanical devices. He was using an analogy. He felt there was something in the clearing that conveyed to him a sense of purpose, perhaps of beauty, and he expressed this sense in the form of a story. Maybe previously he had marvelled at the purposive beauty of a well-tended plot, and that suggested the form of the analogy. He was not saying how the clearing came into existence but expressing his reaction to it and his evaluation of it. He is using figurative, religious language, while his literal-minded friend is talking scientific language, and so he fails to communicate.

It is tempting to conclude that religious language has meaning for those who use it, but is liable to be misunderstood and to fail to communicate in a world that is conditioned to think that truth can be set out only in scientific categories. The matter is, however, more complex than that. Religious people insist that they are not only telling how they feel but saying something about the nature of reality and that their doctrines are saying something about what is the case. Some of them appear to be unaffected by the empirical spirit of science and are able to assert that their talk is to be taken literally and that, if it conflicts with scientific explanations, then the latter are in error. These are the fundamentalists and the literalists who can look on their scriptures as the exact words of their God, believe in the historical nature of their myths, and envisage an almost mechanical relationship between their God and creation.

Others would seem to have a schizophrenic approach, using religious language in a mostly literal way while talking with each other, but using the prevailing empirically-based language at other times, and failing to relate the two or to notice possible discrepancies between them. Furthermore it may not be accurate to make a clear-cut distinction between expressive talk and factual talk and to say that religious language is expressive and evaluative and in no way concerned with stating 'how things are'. We shall need to return to this in the next few pages.

The implication of all this for the teacher of religious education is that he is going to have problems of communication with his pupils, and be liable to be misunderstood by his colleagues and by the general public, both those who are sceptical about religion and those who are keenly connected with it. The pupils, being children of their age, will tend to interpret religious language literally, to think its statements are intended to be factual and historical. This does not seem to occasion trouble with the very young or with adolescents who belong to a fundamentalist religious body, but older pupils who appreciate the significance of the scientific method are inclined to find religious language incomprehensible, to think it is saying something other than it is and to reject it as poor history and worse science. Communication in the classroom breaks down when religion is taught neat, without prior consideration at length of what religion is about and what sort of statements it uses. This is an advanced activity, possible only in the upper forms, which may account for the rejection of religious education by many in the middle of the secondary school.

Pupil misunderstanding and mystification is likely to be shared by colleagues and by many outside school, who will, as a result, have reservations about the wisdom of including religious education in the curriculum. On the other hand, religious bodies, particularly those of a literalist and fundamentalist cast of mind, charge the teacher with dereliction of duty if he does not insist that religious doctrines are concerned with the nature of reality and suggest that he summon up his resolution to overcome pupil resistance, while failing to understand the pedogogical difficulties of what they are asking. If religious education is to maintain a place in the curriculum it has to find a way of commending itself to both these outlooks, and also discover means of assisting pupils to explore the nature of religious language.

Value Statements and Statements of Fact

Once it had been pointed out that religious language is talking in a special way, different from ordinary everyday language and from the empirical statements of science, some attempt had to be made to say what it is talking about, if it was not to be dismissed as insignificant chatter. Various writers have tried to show that it is more than meaningless non-sense. Hare argued that it was not talking about the world, but about our attitude to it, our evaluation of it, and our opinion about how we ought to react to it. He invented a word for it and called it our 'blik' on the world.[8] R. B. Braithwaite thought that religious talk was moral talk, and that religious stories are intended to provide motivation to live up to the ideas expressed by it.[9] I. M. Ramsey put forward the view that religion is a particularly insightful way of looking at experience which could be looked at in other ways as well with equal veracity.[10] For him religious experience is a 'disclosure experience', disclosing something in the natural which goes beyond it. This is the supernatural, which is not anti-natural or contra-natural, but something in the natural itself which is not perceived by objective empirical observation. All three agree that the 'blik', the moral idea or the disclosure carried with it a sense of commitment to live in a particular way.

If these views are accepted the problem of religious language is eased. Religion is talking about human perception, human assessments of experience, and human aspirations to particular lifestyles. The stories and the beliefs that go with religion are explanatory and for hortatory purposes. One does not need, therefore, to ask whether they are true, but whether they perform their function. So in teaching we can explain and justify commitments without having to choose between them and we can turn the learners' question, 'But is it true?', by saying, 'We do not need to ask that question, because religious statements tell us truly about believers' beliefs and attitudes but are not designed to state what is the case in the created world.'

There are, however, difficulties about that position. Will the stories and doctrines fulfil their explanatory and motivating purpose if they are not accepted as true, as related in some way to reality? Will a myth or a belief function if it is known to be only a story or only a belief? If it will, then religion is scarcely more than a self-con-trick.

It is, moreover, difficult to see how it is possible to make any statement about how one evaluates the world and the experiences we have in it without implying some statement about the world as it is. Our evaluation of anything is influenced by what we think it is. For instance, if I say, 'I think this is a good car. I shall commit myself to buying it and I think I shall feel safe when driving it', I do so because I have made certain decisions about the nature of the machine itself, because it has sound engineering, power-assisted brakes, and accurate steering. Similarly with religion; it is difficult to see how it can be a purely evaluative exercise entirely divorced from decisions about the existence or otherwise of God, the nature of that God, the nature of creation and other such matters.

It would seem that religious language is talking about two different things simultaneously, about how the believer assesses experience and about what he takes to be real. Peter Donovan has pointed out how easy it is to slip from one to the other and to confuse the two.

> First, they (religions) are attempting to express deep experiences and emotions and to influence human response and behaviour. Secondly, they are attempting to talk about an elusive and obscure subject matter (whether that be a god or gods, supernatural states of affairs, or mystical levels of consciousness). Oblique figurative language lends itself to the former aim, the arousing of human response. And it can hardly be avoided for the latter, the attempt to speak about the transcendent. The danger is that by succeeding in its first aim religious language can too easily create the impression that the second aim has also been achieved.[11]

This tendency for religious language to start from the subjective and imperceptibly to slide into the objective is the reason why religions propound doctrines which seem patently and objectively true to the believer, but incredibly unverifiable to others. The believer starts by asserting that he looks at life in a particular way because he *believes* this and this to be the case. At this stage it is no more than a belief. The next step is for him to insist that this and this is the case, quite apart from his believing it, and that it should be recognised by all and evaluated as he evaluates it. For instance, if a Christian feels that he is saved because of the death of Jesus, he will say, 'I believe Jesus died for me.' The next stage is to say that Jesus' death had a saving efficacy, *ex opere operato* quite apart from Christian beliefs about it, and to state 'Jesus died for you too', and eventually to arrive at a doctrine that 'Jesus died for the sins of the whole world.' What started as a subjective belief in a relationship has become an apparently objective empirical fact, which will not have that status for those who do not experience the original relationship. There is consequently an ambiguity about religious talk which makes it seem more objective to the believer than to the unbeliever.

This question of whether, mixed up in their belief statements, religions are making assertions about the nature of things is the subject of ongoing debate, and it is not the purpose of this writing to make choice between the two points of view, or to define in detail what religious language is saying. The situation has been briefly outlined because of the effect that debate is likely to have on any attempt to fashion a theory of religious education. Any such attempt has to take into account the existence of two views about the nature of its subject matter. Believing pupils and religious bodies, on the one hand, see it as having some element of assertion about reality, while secularists and unbelieving pupils, on the other hand, regard it as a matter of individual, evaluative, and optional beliefs. How is it to be handled by a teacher without seeming a misrepresentation to one group or the other?

The Problem of Myth

An aspect of religious language which is likely to cause confusion to an age when attitudes have recently been radically changed by a transforming plethora of new discoveries is myth. Religions have an extensive collection of stories which they use mythologically to enshrine some of their deepest apprehensions of what human experience signifies. These stories are culturally conditioned, and most of them have been in use for a long time. They usually belong to cultures that have passed and do not fit the culture that now is. Yet religions go on telling them, and teachers go on teaching about them, even though they are alien to present experience and do not speak to the human spirit as once they did.

The word 'myth' is not being used here in the sense that it is employed in everyday conversation and in popular journalism to mean an untrue story, a fiction, or an unfounded erroneous belief. It is being used to refer to a story used by a religion to express feelings about the significance of the world and of man's place in it, feelings which those who tell the story are convinced are valid, and which can be expressed in no other way.

A religion attempts, among other things, to give to its adherents some notion of the purpose of their experience and of their place in the order of things. The difficulty about this is that purpose, like other abstract notions such as beauty and patriotism, cannot be experienced or defined in its pure essence. It can be expressed only in a symbol or a story. One cannot see beauty – only beauty enshrined in a beautiful object. One cannot see purpose, although one can perhaps see purpose working itself out in practice. To express beauty it is necessary to make a beautiful object. To portray patriotism it is necessary to use a symbol, such as Britannia or Uncle Sam, or tell a story of a patriotic deed. Similarly purpose has to be expressed obliquely, and that is why religions employ stories to retail their convictions about ultimate purpose, and those stories are technically called 'myths'. Bultmann has described the use of myth in these terms:

> The real purpose of myth is not to present an objective picture of the world as it is, but to express man's understanding of himself in the world in which he lives. Myth should be interpreted not cosmologically, but anthropologically, or better still, existentially. Myth speaks of the power or the powers which man supposes he experiences as the ground and limit of his world and of his own activity and suffering. He describes these powers in terms derived from the visible world, with its tangible objects and forces, and from human life, with its feelings, motives, and potentialities . . . He speaks of the other world in terms of this world, and of the gods in terms derived from human life.[12]

The myths that were effective in the pre-scientific age generally described the creation of the world by some more ultimate power and tried to explain why, if the creator was good, his creation included so much imperfection and pain. Often they described the world as a battleground of good and evil forces. When men were uninterested in, and ignorant of, the inherent natural forces of the world in which they lived, but acutely conscious of pain and misfortune, they were likely to describe their world in dramatic terms, similar to those they used to describe personal relationships. Further, knowing little of how matter was modified by its own inherent properties, their chief experience of rearranging the pieces of the world were their own activities of building and making and planting, in which they engaged with conscious purpose. It was but a small step to invent a story of how the whole universe was similarly moulded by a gigantic, purposive being, and to ascribe the manner in which creation modified itself in the form of growth and gravity and meteorological manifestations, not to forces in the world itself, but to the activities of the purposive creator. Observation that disaster and suffering were often caused by human decisions would lead to the view that pains and misfortunes that resulted from non-human agencies were the planned product of supernatural forces.

Myths to account for evil take two forms. There is the Platonic one that the world we know is an imperfect expression in matter of a more real and perfect world of ideas; our world gets its imperfection from the intractability of the matter which forms it, and is struggling to overcome that handicap and achieve perfection. The second form of the myth is the Persian one, which was adopted first by the Jews and then taken on by the Christians, that the universe is a three-tiered affair. In the uppermost tier, usually called Heaven, live the creator and attendant good spirits; in the lowest tier live the evil influences; and the middle tier is the known world which both good and bad spirits seek to influence and to dominate. The world in general, and human minds in particular, are a kind of battle ground between them, and in the course of the battle one may rise to heaven or sink to hell. This accounts, on the one hand, for disaster and evil, and, on the other hand, for the experience of beauty and for aspiration to the good.

These stories, that have served as myths in the past, have decisively influenced the form of religious doctrines. With such a world view it is not difficult to believe in a good creator God, struggling to establish his purpose in the face of opposition from evil forces, and to believe that he makes that purpose known to men by revelations through prophets, avatars and incarnations, and that he occasionally intrudes dramatically and miraculously into his creation to modify it when it gets out of hand. Those sorts of doctrines accord easily with the older mythological world view.

Though myths are human constructions to help us understand and make sense of the world and our place in it, they must not conflict with practical experience. To be effective in helping man to come to a satisfying theory about the total nature of things, they have to be believed to be true. They have to be taken for statements of fact, and this is unlikely if they contradict experience. It would be difficult for us today to believe in a myth that the world was created by one god slaying another and hacking his body in pieces,[13] because our experience of the world is such that it is inexplicable as a hacked-up body. When a situation arises in which those who are using a particular myth are forced to compare it with their experience of reality and find that it does not fit, they are forced to recognise that the myth is not a factual description, and it is shattered for them. That is what seems to have been happening in the past century, to the detriment of the old myths. Since by scientific and detached investigation we have had a new kind of experience of the world, stories of an anthropomorphic creator God do not square with it; now we know more of the causes of pain and disaster, the idea that they are due to a conflict of opposing good and evil spirits seems over-fanciful. Thus, even though these myth-stories may still have some hold on popular imagination and appear superficially in social discourse, to the scientific mind they are historical relics, as curious and irrelevant as the Greek and Roman myths, which were discarded long ago. As a result the religious doctrines that are expressed in terms of them become difficult to believe and even vaguely ludricrous.

As a result of this, the myths which in the past have been the accepted mode for making sense of the totality of experience can no longer be used in public discourse. Politics, commerce, industry, the many forms of scholarship, and social organisations employ other models to structure their thinking. Yet the older myths are still used by religious people, both in their individual thinking and when they congregate for discussion of their beliefs and for worship. Like religion itself, they have become privatised, and in a private context they still seem to have meaning. For some, such as the more conservative religious groups and the new Jesus cults, they retain their old force, and can be talked about at all times, often to the mystification of those who do not share their views. Others talk of them only when they are in a religious milieu, among like-minded believers, and use other methods of expression in general conversation. Consequently such myths are 'in-talk', appropriate for communication within the circle of believers, but which do not have the same significance, or make the same sense, to those outside, whose world view is expressed in other terms.

Perhaps at this point we may enquire what are the myths of today? This is a question difficult to answer, because, as pointed out above, myths, to fulfil their explanatory function, must look like descriptions of reality and it is not easy for a culture to recognise what its own myths are. Possibly one might say that Freud's attempt to explain the human psyche in terms of the Ego, the Super-Ego and the Id is a myth, and that the Marxist account of history and social relationships as a class war is another. The scientist's picturing of the atom as a group of differing spheres revolving round an axis seems to perform a mythical function. Perhaps the most powerful mythical notion of our time (this is put forward as a tentative suggestion) is the idea that the universe is a collection of atoms subject to energetic forces and that all past experience can be explained in terms of this and all future events predicted from knowledge of it. Laplace put this in an extreme form when he wrote:

> We ought, then, to regard the present state of the universe as the effect of its antecedent state and the cause of the state that is to follow. An intelligence, who for a given instant should be acquainted with all the forces by which Nature is animated and with the several positions of the entities composing it, if further his intellect were vast enough to submit those data to analysis . . . the future as well as the past would be present to his eyes.[14]

One is aware that the scientific ideas implied by this are now old-fashioned, and that later theories of reality and of the nature of scientific investigation take a less confident line, and it may be that these mythical ideas will be shattered in their turn by being shown to conflict with human experience of the environment. The point at issue is that this world view or 'blik' is influencing the thinking of wide sections of the population who are not in the forefront of scientific research and is still fuelling a good deal of intellectual activity.[15] More important for our purpose, it is also predominant in school classrooms.

If the prevailing myths influence the form in which religious doctrines are expounded, we have to ask what forms of doctrines will accord with these modern myths. Certainly doctrines which maintain that ultimate reality lies outside, and exists in opposition to, created matter, and that ultimate truth originates from uninvestigable supernatural beings, who occasionally inrupt into the created world in ways which conflict with its self-determined workings, and reveal their nature by mystical means, are not going to look convincing. What may replace that cosmology is not yet clear. It is the task of theologians to explain how old truth can be redefined in terms consonant with new knowledge. Their attempts to do so cause scholarly controversy, as in the debate that followed the publication of a set of essays under the title of *The Myth of God Incarnate*,[16] but have so far had little influence upon the beliefs and the talk of rank and file believers. Nevertheless, the unprecedented expansion of human knowledge is placing all religions in ferment, and any religion that is not prepared 'to go on adapting itself into something which can be believed – believed by honest and thoughtful people',[17] is likely to be taken seriously only by a dwindling few.

The mythological ferment – one might even call it crisis – that is afflicting religions necessarily has implications for religious education. The teacher is faced with a situation in which some still accept traditional myths as factual statements, and wish him to teach them as such, while others regard them as discarded, pre-scientific fantasies, and do not wish them to be taught at all. The theological restatement of them gives him little help, because it is incomplete and is too abstruse for the understanding of any except the oldest and brightest pupils. Pupils themselves react differently to myths, since they include those for whom the traditional stories retain meaning and those for whom they do not. In such confused circumstances the teacher has to choose between a number of procedures. Firstly, he can try to teach the stories and interpret them as though they were still unquestioned, in which case he will be communicating to that section of the class who are able to respond to such an outlook. Secondly, he can teach the stories as things which religious people 'used to believe', and see his work as an antiquarian and historical study. Thirdly, he can teach the stories as ones which people who happen to be religious use in their thinking and in their worship, but that may produce a backlash by giving the impression that religion is an activity of the peculiarly old-fashioned and not worth learning about. Fourthly, he may institute an enquiry into what the myths meant to those who used them in the past, into what meaning religious people find in them today, into how far the truths they expressed are still valid and, if they are, into how they can be expressed in believable terms in the present. This could lead to a discussion and an appreciation of the need of any culture to make sense of its world, and of the impossibility of grasping that sense except in imaginative story form. This could be related to the non-religious myths, similar to those mentioned above, and pupils invited to consider the mythology of the scientific world and what it contributes to human understanding. A study of that sort might help maturer pupils to get nearer to the heart of religion and to see its doctrines as more than a collection of improbable assertions. For the younger ones, it might be sufficient for them to enjoy the myths provided they are helped to realise that they are significant of deeper meaning than the story alone. If that is pointed out to them it may prevent them scornfully dismissing the stories before they are mature enough to think at depth about their meaning and function.

In an age when religions, and particularly the Christian religion, are becoming aware of the problems connected with their mythological stories and attempting to reinterpret them, religious education is not going to be straightforward. The literalist approach to religious stories, though it may be welcomed by the conservative, will probably in the long run promote confusion and incomprehension. Some restructuring of the syllabus to include study of the mythological nature and effect of religious stories is needed.

NOTES

1 Department of Education and Science, *A Language for Life*, H.M.S.O., 1975, p.190.
2 Harold Rosen, 'Towards a language policy across the curriculum' (1971, pp.134–5). It is convenient to accept this distinction for the moment, but it will be argued later in the chapter that the confusion arises from the fact that the two categories are not entirely separable.
3 Properly used, the word 'sin' has no meaning for an atheist.
4 Rosen, *op.cit.*, p.133.
5 A. J. Ayer (1946).
6 The hyphen is used because, in the first instance, the Logical Positivists meant that religious statements are not sense testable rather than that they were nonsense in the popular meaning of the word. But they do not appear to think the distinction has any significance.
7 The story is too well known to need repeating fully, but Flew's version of it can be found in A. Flew and A. MacIntyre (eds) (1955, p.96).
8 In Flew and MacIntyre, *op.cit.*, pp.99–103.
9 In R. B. Braithwaite (1955).
10 In I. M. Ramsey, (1957).
11 Peter Donovan, (1976, p.10).
12 H. W. Bartsch (ed.) (1953, p.10).
13 As in one version of the Norse myth of Ymir and Buri.
14 Quoted in C. E. M. Joad (1942, p.235f.).
15 It lies behind attempts to demonstrate that human thinking is determined by antecedent cause rather than free reflection; behind the confidence that social relationships can be understood by statistical investigation; behind the contention that politics are ultimately conditioned by inexorable economic and social forces; and it is the presupposition of many disciplines studied in the academic world.
16 John Hick (ed.) (1977).
17 Hick, *op.cit.*, p.ix.

7 The Relation of Religious Education and Moral Education

Since 1965 there has been a strongish movement to introduce into British schools a new subject called Moral Education. Sometimes attempts are made to justify this new subject by claiming that it is needed to fill the lacuna left by the failure of religious education. Formerly, it is maintained, society was sufficiently religious, or more specifically Christian, for it to be able to teach religion to its young, and, since that religion included definite ideas of what constituted moral action, and also a belief in certain rewards and punishments that served to motivate to moral action, children were made moral by first being made religious. Now, however, pupils are not always receiving instruction about religion in schools, and are not responding so strongly to that instruction when it is given; consequently they are receiving no guidance on right action and something ought to be done to make good the defect. Even if we feel no longer justified in persuading pupils to accept religion, we must somehow persuade them to accept the virtues that previously have been associated with religion.

Those with no great love of religion have been active in their support of moral education, seeing it as a possible substitute for the teaching about religion in schools, to which they have ideological objections. As a result, religious education and moral education are sometimes presented as though they were rivals or alternatives. This, however, may be too simplistic a view. The relation between religion and morals is a complex one, both historically and philosophically. The case for the absolute divorce of the two is by no means clear to everyone. Furthermore it is possible that the present confusion about how they should be treated in schools has its roots in uncertainties that afflict human thinking at this point in history. The pressures that prevent the general acceptance of religious ideas may also be pressures that prevent the discerning and teaching of any widely-accepted moral ideas. An examination of this may lead to clarification of the relationship, if any, between religious education and moral education. Are they two sides of the same study? Or are they completely different matters? Can we have both, or must we choose either one or the other? Or is there a fundamental connection between them, even though there may be practical reasons for conducting them as separate educational activities at present?

It is impossible to consider such a question without immediately asking what is meant by the word 'moral', for there seem to be two ways in which the word is used. The first sense in which it is used respects its derivation from the Latin word *mores*, and makes it refer to the customs that any society demands that its members observe. This is perhaps a superficial use, for it implies that moral action has no deeper justification than that society, at the moment, has agreed to ask for it. At another time it might ask for something different, and other societies could well have completely different conceptions of what constitutes moral living. Morality is, then, relative to what a society perceives to be conducive to its own well-being.

On this view, moral education will consist of telling the young how their elders have decided they shall behave and seeing that they are trained to obey by habit. Hirst has called such a concept of moral education a 'primitive' one, 'for it clearly expresses the view of education a primitive tribe might have when it seeks to pass on to the next generation its rituals, its ways of farming and so on, according to its own customs and beliefs. Whatever is held by the group to be true and valuable, simply because it is held to be true and valuable, is what is passed on, so that it comes to be held as true and valuable by others in their turn.'[1]

The other way in which the term 'moral' is used is to refer to something more profound than human choice or human custom on the theory that there is something outside human decision and preference that makes an action right or wrong. There is, on this view, something imperative and 'given' about morals which man has to discover and to which he ought to strive to conform. To put it in other words, there is something deep in the nature of things which provides the criteria for moral choice. Moral decision is, on this view, more objective than a society's wishes and customs, so that when two societies differ in their *mores* we can decide which is the better and say that one is more moral than the other by reference to this deeper concept. For instance, when a Christian culture says that life is sacred and to be preserved at all cost and an Aztec culture says that is not so and that human sacrifice is desirable, they cannot both be right. One will be nearer in accord with the morality basic to the universe and therefore more moral than the other.

The question now arises of what is that deeper something to which appeal can be made to adjudicate in cases of moral uncertainty? Is it something in the way the world is made, something in 'the grain of the universe'? Or does it reside in some personal creative intelligence which made the universe with that grain? Or is it something in the logic of thinking which implies that there are certain values which have to be respected if we are to talk about morals at all? These are fundamental questions, because the answers we give to them will determine:

(a)   how we distinguish between moral and immoral action;
(b)   how we think teaching about morals should be undertaken in schools;
(c)   the relation between religion and morality, and, by implication, the relation between religious education and moral education.

A religiously-minded person will, of course, support the second of those two views of morality that have been described. It is of the essence of religions to include belief that there is some principle, be it the Holy Trinity, Allah, or Brahma, from which the rationale of existence and experience is derived. That principle has determined the grain of the universe and is the ground of the moral law. Action in accord with the will (or nature) of that principle is considered to be moral, and other action designated immoral and sinful. For religious believers the road to right action is to discover the will of their God (either by reflection on experience or by giving heed to revelations of that will) and to summon the resolution to live in accord with it.

Here, then, we have one simple relationship between religious education and moral education. Religion entails morality, and to give a person a religion includes giving him the appropriate moral training. That is why, in the past, when religious education was thought of as teaching pupils the Christianity of their forefathers, moral education ensued. It was moral education of a particular sort, namely Christian moral education. It will be objected now that this is insufficient, and that moral education cannot any longer be conducted in such a way in Britain, because not everyone is prepared to accept Christian morality as the only one to be considered, and because religious education is no longer regarded as making pupils religious. The point at issue is that, although it is claimed to be possible to construct systems of moral education without reference to religious ideas, yet religious education will be doing something towards moral education because it will involve critical examination of the moral ideas of the religion being studied.

Since there is this essential connection between a religion and its associated moral system, the present demand for a moral education without reference to religious ideas can be seen as one aspect of the rejection of religion by the contemporary world. Many people are not prepared to accept the moral criteria advocated by a religion, either because they doubt the veracity of the theology on which it is based, or because they notice that different religions and ideologies produce different, and sometimes conflicting, moral systems. It consequently seems necessary to look for some principles that will guide moral choice without involving metaphysical and mythologically expressed beliefs which are difficult to accept.

That is not to say that there are not many religious people who sincerely try to live up to the morality that their religion entails. Indeed there are. But the prevailing secular cast of thought reduces religion from a public to a private matter.

> The more secular society becomes, the more its social life and institutions become determined by considerations that are acceptable to all, no matter what their attitude to religious belief. In so far as religious and non-religious people can agree about social principles, religious questions can be regarded as a private personal matter . . . Such privatisation is increasingly the mark of our own secular society, in which the widest range of attitudes to religious beliefs is acceptable, provided they are never allowed to determine public issues.[2]

Moral education is, however, concerned with public issues. It tries to train children to make sensible judgments about behaviour which is likely to affect those around them. It discusses private moral decisions in so far as they impinge on the happiness and convenience of other people and are, to that extent, public issues. If, therefore, religion is a private hobby, unconnected with public issues, then its beliefs will not be acceptable as a basis for moral discussion and for moral education. Some other agreed method of deciding what morals shall be taught must be found. Much of the research into moral education, such as that of John Wilson at the Farmington Trust and that of Peter McPhail which produced the *Lifeline* material for classroom use, has had the stipulated purpose of finding a non-religious basis for moral teaching. How far it has succeeded is difficult to assess.

What such projects have done is to come up with a newish conception of moral education. Previously it was thought of as acquainting pupils with the accepted and approved moral criteria, and motivating them to apply those criteria in their own moral choices and to carry them out in practice. This process is now deprecatingly described as moralising. Present thinking doubts whether our society has any publicly accepted and agreed criteria, and so sees the subject as helping pupils make sincere, informed, autonomous choices without trying to tell them what values, apart from a democratic benevolence, should apply in making those choices. It maintains that the teaching should help pupils to understand that living involves making certain decisions and that those decisions affect the quality both of our own life and those of others (McPhail), assist them to appreciate the psychological attitudes that underlie decision making (Farmington), and encourage them to grow into autonomous, morally responsible and self-determining individuals (Kohlberg, Wilson, and others), but in no way to pre-empt their choice or to advocate any particular kind of morality. This may be the best we can do in a morally uncertain age, but it is not what the average person means when he asks for moral education in schools.

> The concern of society, at least as expressed by its more vocal representatives, appears to be with the immediate control of unruly pupils and with a reduction of the incidence of theft, violence, vandalism and the like.[3]

This new view of moral education is separating it clearly from religion. Religion is concerned with the content of morality; the new moral education is concerned with the freedom and rationality of moral choice but not with the content of it. The values that a pupil, or anyone for that matter, applies in deciding his actions is, like religion, a private matter, and so, like religion, does not come into the scope of moral education as at present frequently conceived.

These are the movements of thought that have tended to make a division between religious education and moral education. The crux of the discussion is whether or not moral criteria can be discovered and defined without reference to any kind of belief system whatever. Perhaps it will help if we look at the theories that are held of the basis of ethical action and note how far they imply religious belief. There are three main ones which seem to be employed in the on-going discussion about moral education in schools.

The View that Morals depend on Religious Belief

Those who hold this view think that God is the source of moral values; moral action is action taken in accord with his will; action not in accord with that will is immoral and sinful. On this view morals can be taught only after religious education has taken place, and a particularly confessional type of religious education, too.

This view is not without its difficulty. Critics of it ask what the justification is for asserting that what God wills is good. The answer is, 'Because God is good.' This implies a concept of goodness against which God can be measured to test whether or not he is good. The origin of morality is outside God and therefore the theory is self-contradictory. It is based on an act of faith (a commitment to a line of action which cannot be justified rationally) and is possible only for those with a deeply religious outlook. Those who take this point of view are saying, 'This is what I think my God commands, I commit myself to it in trust and faith, and do not need to argue it out any further.' But those without such a deeply religious outlook will feel a need to argue it out further.

The View that Ethical Theory is derived from the Nature of Things

This maintains that there are certain principles inherent in the nature of things which are pressing upon human beings when they make moral decisions. It should be possible to discover those things by investigation, to define them, and to get them accepted by all rational persons, irrespective of their religious beliefs. Morality, then, need have nothing to do with beliefs, and ethics is a descriptive as well as a normative science. It should be possible, having isolated those discoverable principles, to teach them in schools. Needless to say this theory has much attraction for an age which places great reliance on empirical data and regards investigation of the material universe as the safest road to truth.

Crudely expressed this theory is nothing more than the 'grain of the universe' theory without God. The religious man says God made the universe with a certain grain and that if we are to be moral we must respect it and live along with it and not against it. The theory under discussion accepts the grain but repudiates any speculation as to why it is there. It may not, however, be the less true for that reason.

One cannot help wondering, all the same, why, if there are discernable principles of morality built into the universe, how it is that philosophers, after 2,500 years at least of moral theorising, have not been able to discover them and agree upon them. One would have thought we should have hit upon them by now and made morals an exact science, free of debate and difference of opinion. Yet those who claim to have found objective moral principles usually describe them in such generalised terms as to make it difficult to apply them in a precise way to choice of action in particular cases. For instance, the Social Morality Council's 'National Plan for Moral Education', published in 1978, maintained that there are some generally agreed moral principles but was hesitant to say what they are beyond general decency and care for others.

The theory is presented in a more subtle way by R. S. Peters, for whom moral action is that for which good reasons can be given.

> Morality, then, is concerned with what there are reasons for doing or not doing, for bringing into or removing from existence.[4]

In order to give reasons for actions it is necessary to appeal to some higher-order principles which 'provide very general criteria of relevance for justifying particular rules and for making exceptions in particular cases'. Professor Peters states what he thinks those higher-order principles to be, and justifies them as being more than personal or culturally conditioned preferences. They are demanded by the nature of things, since it is impossible to talk about reasons for actions without involving them.

> The higher-order principles which, in my view, are capable of some sort of rational justification, are those of impartiality, truth-telling, liberty, and the consideration of interests. For

these, I would argue, are presupposed by the very activity of giving reasons in practical discourse.[5]

It is interesting that Professor Peters states that he is presenting here both a view and an argument, for it raises the question of whether these particular higher-order principles are based on opinion or on logical necessity. The latter is claimed, but is the claim valid? There are large areas of the world which construct their *mores* on other considerations, and if we accept Professor Peters's argument we have to condemn them as immoral, as blind to the moral principles in the nature of things. It is just possible, however, that culture has an effect on our perception of higher-order principles and that the ones mentioned above would not seem so necessary a part of reasonable discourse outside western civilization. Are they as objective and judgment-free as they seem?

To put the matter another way, the higher-order principles usually appealed to in a liberal democratic culture presuppose that the welfare, or more often the well-being, of human beings is the basis of moral action. Good deeds are those that promote human development, human self-realisation, human comfort and human happiness. Rarely do they mention that perhaps the universe may demand sacrifice or suffering or endurance, although such things are admired as a sort of unfortunate occasional inevitable necessity. One therefore wonders whether this approach to morality is objective in essence, or whether it is dependent upon certain beliefs about man and his happiness being the measure of all things. Perhaps that is why it appeals especially to humanists and humanitarians.

One is not saying that the attempt to achieve a moral system by searching for principles in the nature of things is foolish. Given the temper of the time it is probably as good a way of reaching moral agreement as any other. One is, however, pointing out that at the root of it there may be certain value judgments and that it may be no more belief-free than the moral system that proceeds from a religion.

The View that Moral Talk is the Dignifying of Personal Preferences

There is a view that would look on all talk on the basis of morality as unnecessary. It regards moral talk as an oblique, and possibly pompous, way of expressing personal preferences. Morality is a kind of emotion with which we dignify those preferences. If you say, 'This action is good,' all you are saying is, 'I approve of this action and intend to do it, and I think you should approve of it too.' Ethical decisions are really subjective choices. R. M. Hare put this view sophisticatedly in his *Language of Morals*[6] when he maintains that you justify a moral choice by showing it to be in line with the way of life to which you are committed. It will be necessary to look at this view again later, but for the moment it may suffice to point out that it makes morals an individual matter. The only way that this view can reach the degree of public consensus that makes discussion about morals and moral education possible is by arriving at agreement on manners of life. To reach agreement a supporter of this view would have to say, 'I approve of committing myself to this manner of life; you should approve of a similar way of life; then we can both resolve moral dilemmas in a similar way and act in identical fashion.'

There are two objections to this view. The first is that it concerns what we think to be right and not what may, in fact, be right. On such a view two opposing decisions could each be equally moral. Suppose I say that chastity is moral, I am only saying that I approve of it and mean to be chaste. Another may say he sees nothing wrong in fornication and that he is committed to a life of promiscuity. On the theory under discussion we could both claim to be acting morally. But suppose there were a rightness and wrongness beyond our opinions. (I am not saying there is, merely that there might be.) If so, this theory doesn't get to the bottom of the matter and produces no moral guidance. It only asserts individual preferences. The second objection is that if we are talking about personal preference, why not say so? Why introduce the vocabulary of moral and immoral, right and wrong, ought and ought not, if more direct terms like, I approve, I am going to, or I am not going to, would suffice?

Does this view have any connection with religion? On first glance, and as usually expounded, it does not. Yet it involves 'a way of life to which you are committed', and commitment is a concept that plays a large part in religious thought. It may, therefore, be worth while looking at this more closely in our attempt to clarify the connection between religious education and moral education. This may help us to escape from the impasse in which we seem to have arrived, where the religious man feels that morality is fundamentally related to religious beliefs and the non-religious man sees no connection at all, but agrees with R. B. Braithwaite who, in his essay *An Empiricist's View of Religious Belief*,[7] puts forward the suggestion that religious statements are moral statements dressed up in story form in order to motivate those who tell and hear the stories to act according to their ideals. Perhaps we may find a way forward if we examine the nature of moral choice, and ask about the sense of commitment and the feeling of obligation that accompany it.

The Ingredients of a Moral Choice

The fact that we call certain choices moral ones presupposes that there are other ones to which the word does not apply, practical choices, financial choices, aesthetic choices, and so on. These latter, under appropriate conditions, may also have a moral element, but what is it that causes certain decisions to be singled out and labelled moral?

There are a number of obvious characteristics. In the first place the choice has to be concerned with a fairly weighty matter and have some fairly serious consequences. Some choices (for example, whether when I polish my shoes, I polish the left one before the right or vice versa) are too trivial to be called moral. Secondly, the choice has to be a free one. If a man is not free, if he is under external compulsion, we do not hold him morally responsible for his decisions in quite the same way, nor do we make moral judgments about actions which the doer cannot help doing. For instance, if you are helping to lift a heavy box and it is too much for your strength so that you drop it on your neighbour's toe, you won't expect to be held morally culpable of his hurt as you would have done if you had dropped it deliberately to pay off some old score you had against him. Thirdly, the doer must be responsible for his choice. A person who is incapacitated mentally, so that he does not understand the implications of his decisions, is held to have diminished moral responsibility. Fourthly, to make it liable to full moral assessment a choice has to be made with adequate knowledge of the facts connected with it and of the likely outcome. Insufficient evidence removes from a choice some of its moral weight. For example, suppose I wish to warn a stranger to get out of the way of an approaching car which he has not noticed, I have to choose whether to warn him by sound or by action. Normally I would shout at him and it would suffice. But if, unknown to me, he were stone deaf, I should have made a wrong choice, but not one that most people would say was highly immoral.

All these considerations would apply, however, to many other choices. One hopes that practical decisions about how one's house is repaired, how one's finances are looked after, how one's tax is worked out and so on are all made freely, responsibly and on adequate evidence. What really sets a moral choice apart and qualifies it to be called moral is the sense of obligation that goes with it. The chooser feels that something is pressing upon him to choose in a certain way and that an unpleasant feeling, called conscience, could be aroused if he ignores it. From whence does this feeling of 'I ought' arise?

It will be convenient here to return to the idea of a moral act being one that is in accord with the manner of life to which the doer is committed. If a person is committed to a certain style it will follow that he will feel an obligation to live up to it, and under some pressure to act in accord with it. We can link this with the view of Allport that conscience is the uncomfortable feeling that follows an action that is out of keeping with one's ego-image.[8] There is, however, the question of how one comes on a manner of life or acquires an ego-image in the first place. These would seem to depend on certain opinions about the significance of experience, about what is ultimately important or 'real', about what kind of animal man is and what kind of life he has a right to expect, and about how far individuals are responsible for the created world and for helping others to achieve the ideal life. Answers to such questions, mixed in varying proportions, condition the manner of life or the ego-image of the individual. It is not suggested that everyone is earnestly asking those questions and solemnly answering them, or consciously and conscientiously constructing a manner of life. Much of it is done subconsciously, and many are influenced by the culture in which they have been reared, by the customs they find around them, and by the assumptions they have unreflectively made. The point is that, however acquired, there are behind manners of life, ego-images and moral decisions certain opinions or beliefs about the nature of life and of humanity.

This may be put in a more practical way. When a question of conduct arises it can usually be answered, in the first place, by a statement. That statement can be made the subject of a further question, to be answered by yet another statement. The process can go on for a while, but eventually a question is reached which cannot be answered by a statement. This is an 'ultimate' question, to which it is possible to respond only by an opinion or a belief, or a working hypothesis. Here is an example:

> Ought I to play golf?
> No, I cannot afford it.
> Why cannot I afford it?
> Because I have a family to support, which must have prior claim on my resources.
> Why should I be concerned with supporting a family?
> Because a man ought to accept his responsibilities.
> Why should he do so?
> Because man should be a responsible animal.
> Why should he?
> I don't know. He just ought. Man is like that.

Or again:

> Shall I call on my grandfather to take him out for a drink?
> Yes, it will cheer him up.
> Why should I cheer up my grandfather?
> Because people ought to be happy.
> Why ought people to be happy?
> I don't know, I just believe they ought.

These not very serious examples illustrate how in the chain of argument to justify a particular choice of action there is a transition from factual statements to belief or opinion statements, and under moral choices and moral systems there is a substructure of belief.

Religious people can always ask one more question in these sequences than people who are not religious. In the above examples they might state that man should be responsible and happy because God intends him to be so. The ultimate question then is, 'Why does God intend that?', to be answered by, 'He just does.' That is why to the believer morality is inextricably bound up with his faith. Yet the non-believer is also making an act of faith, or being influenced by a belief, even though the belief may not involve theism.

If moral decisions depend in this way on assumptions or beliefs about the nature of ourselves as human beings, about the nature of the world in which we live, and about the responsibilities we have to the world and to our fellows, then a moral education that does not recognise the connection between beliefs and decisions is going to be superficial. It is not being suggested that moral education should try to tell pupils what assumptions they are to make in adopting a manner of life and in making their moral choices, merely that they ought to know, by the end of school life, that they are forced to make assumptions and to be critically aware of what assumptions they are in fact making.

There is here a plain link between moral education and religious education. If religious education includes a study of the beliefs that groups of people hold and of how they respond to them, it can be imparting an appreciation of the inevitable connection between beliefs and moral decision as well as a consciousness of what pupils themselves believe and of how their beliefs are influencing their response to problems of conduct. In this way the two subjects can feed into and reinforce each other. As ever, it depends on how religious education is envisaged and conducted, but instead of regarding religious education and moral education as potential divorcees it might be wiser to look on them as Siamese twins.

NOTES

1   P. H. Hirst (1974, p. 80).
2   Hirst, *op. cit.*, p. 3.
3   D. Wright in his editorial to *The Journal of Moral Education*, 6, 1, October 1976, p. 4.
4   R. S. Peters, 'Reason and habit; the paradox of moral education' (Peters, 1963, p. 48).
5   Peters, *op.cit.*, p. 51.
6   R. M. Hare (1952).
7   R. B. Braithwaite (1955).
8   See G. W. Allport (1955, pp. 68–74).

8 The Problem of Indoctrination

There was a time when a teacher would have been proud to be described as a good indoctrinator. Augustine, Aquinas and even Arnold would have seen little wrong in indoctrinating. For an indoctrinator was originally one who imparted doctrine, and doctrine, when used in the meaning implied by its classical roots, is only another word for teaching. So to be an indoctrinator was to be a successful teacher. It was, however, taken for granted that the doctrine was true, and that the teacher was not trying to impart ideas that were false.

Indoctrination has now become a reprehensible activity because we attach a different meaning to the word 'doctrines'. That term is no longer extended to all teachings, but confined to theories, especially the beliefs of religious bodies and the speculative opinions of political parties. The teacher dealing with politics or religion is particularly liable to be called an indoctrinator, an appellation which he regards not as a compliment but as a charge to be dreaded. It is therefore important that the religious education teacher should understand what is meant by the term 'indoctrination' and the ways in which his subject is vulnerable to the charge of being indoctrination.

What is Indoctrination?

The preceding paragraph has already given us one clue to the meaning of the term – indoctrination has to do with the study of theories, with an area in which there may be differences of opinions, even disputes. Yet the term is not frequently applied to attempts in social conversation to persuade others to agree with one's point of view, or to debates in Parliament or wrangles in pubs. To be an indoctrinator the person trying to impart the doctrines must be in a position of authority which influences the learner. At worst he is a brainwasher, who tries to change his victim's beliefs by methods which are morally indefensible because the victim cannot resist them or make rational judgments about what is being imparted. At best he is abusing his authority, especially if he is a teacher, whose duty it is to lead pupils to understanding and rationality; instead he is attempting to influence them without regard for either understanding or rationality. Patricia Smart has pointed out that indoctrination is the use of questionable means to cause a pupil to reach a premature opinion.

> To talk of indoctrination is to suggest that the teacher uses unfair means to induce the child to come to conclusions which he himself intends him to make, but which the subject matter does not necessarily demand.[1]

Another characteristic of indoctrination is that it is something that takes place over a period of time. One might call a teacher stupidly ignorant if he tried to get a class to accept an untruth, or ill-advised if he tried to impart a belief with which one disagrees, but one would not call him an indoctrinator unless he continued to do this over a space of time in order to change the attitudes, the judgments, or the opinions of his class.

An over-simple definition of indoctrination is that it is teaching without making available to the learners the reasons for what is taught or the reasons why they should accept it. It is over-simple because young children cannot always understand the reasons for those things that it is necessary for them to learn. The infant has to take his parents' and his teachers' word for a number of things if he is to acquire rapidly the ability to communicate and to avoid physical harm. And education would be a more tedious and lengthy thing than it is if every teacher had to give reasons for everything that he includes in his lessons. There has to be an element of trust in the teacher's own knowledge, but this does not mean he is an indoctrinator provided he is careful in choosing the material that he requires the pupils to accept on his say-so, and if reasons for it are produced when asked for and when the pupils are able to understand them.

It may help at this point to consider some of the definitions of indoctrination that have been put forward. J. P. White in his essay 'Indoctrination' suggests that it is teaching with the intention that the pupil will believe what is taught in such a way that nothing will subsequently shake his belief.[2] This focuses on the intention and method of the teacher rather than on the content of the teaching, and may, for that reason, be too wide a definition. The health teacher tries to impart the unshakable belief that teeth should be brushed and exercise taken regularly and that is not regarded as indoctrinatory. Unshakable faith may be one result of indoctrination, but if there are some things about which unshakable faith is acceptable then reference to content is required if the definition is to be precise. Snook tries to provide for this when he writes:

> I suggest that the following provides a necessary and sufficient condition of indoctrination: A person indoctrinates P (a proposition or set of propositions) if he teaches with the intention that the pupil or pupils believe P regardless of the evidence.[3]

Basil Mitchell, in his appendix to *The Fourth R*,[4] places emphasis on the content involved when he describes indoctrination as teaching as true that which is disputatious. These definitions imply that content, method and teacher intention are all involved in certain ways. They need to be looked at separately to see what each is contributing.

How is Indoctrination Achieved?

Some teaching content (religion, politics, morals, for example) is more susceptible of being described as the subject of indoctrination than others (mathematics, science, for example). This might suggest that it is the selection of lesson material that makes the difference between acceptable teaching and unacceptable conditioning. Teachers have to deal with various types of content, some of which are more likely than others to lead to indoctrination.

(a) There are facts, such as the situation of Cape Horn on the southernmost tip of the American continent, the composition of water out of two parts of hydrogen and one part of oxygen, the agreed relationships of mathematics and the presence of four Gospels in the orthodox Christian Bible. These are things that can be publicly verified, to which contrary evidence cannot reasonably be produced, and of which knowledge can be imparted unshakably to pupils without arousing the charge of indoctrination.

(b)   There are theories generally accepted in the community, such as kindness is desirable, honesty is the foundation of civilised converse, good health is better than bad, people should be free to choose their own government, and so on. These are not so publicly and compulsively demonstrable as facts but, provided everyone in the community subscribes to them, they can be taught without being classed as indoctrination. A visitor from another culture, where such theories were not taken for granted, would, however, so regard them.

(c)   There are falsehoods, which may, as the result of ignorance or accident, get occasionally included in the lesson. White uses the teaching that Melbourne is the capital of Australia[5] as an illustration of indoctrination and Snook agrees that, if this were taught, it would be indoctrination. One might add that this notion could be imparted only by indoctrinatory methods since contrary evidence could easily be produced. Even so, one is less inclined to call this indoctrination as teaching what is patently known to be false.

(d)   There are theories and beliefs which are held by a sufficient proportion of people to prevent them being thought completely cranky, but not by others – that is, the sort of things that Basil Mitchell calls disputatious. Those who hold them think there is evidence in support of them. Those who do not hold them either question this or think there is contrary evidence. This is the type of content that may be taught in indoctrinatory fashion. If the teacher presents only the favourable evidence and hides, or unfairly decries, contradictory considerations so that the pupils are likely to arrive at a prejudiced conclusion, then he is indoctrinating by selection of content.

The discussion so far would seem to lead to the idea that indoctrination is the peculiar use of particular material. However, something more is needed, for to be thoroughly indoctrinated the pupils have to reach a prejudiced conclusion and, in addition, be so conditioned as to refuse to review it when other evidence appears. If they are reasonable persons this is possible only if they are so emotionally attached to their view as to reject the new evidence. Method, therefore, is involved. The teacher, by over-enthusiasm, by undue use of authority, or by angry disapproval of questioning, arouses emotions in those he teaches so that they identify with the teaching, feel defensive of it, and experience repulsion, insecurity and even anger when objections are made or other and conflicting ideas are presented.

There remains the matter of intention. Presumably if a teacher is consciously indoctrinating he has the intention of doing so because he thinks it is in the interest of the pupils or in the interest of some organisation to which he belongs, or because he considers it will advance the establishment of a social and political order that he thinks desirable. There is, however, difficulty in making intention a sufficient condition of indoctrination. What if the teacher intends to indoctrinate but, because of the resistance of the pupils or his own lack of technique, fails to do so? Is a failed indoctrinator an indoctrinator? There is similar difficulty with making intention a necessary condition. It would not function in the case of one who was so attached to a theory or belief that he did not realise its disputatious nature, or recognise the evidence against it, and, as a result, indoctrinated without realising he was doing so. He would lack the intention, but would be an indoctrinator none the less. Anyone who has been himself indoctrinated will be in this position and so will inevitably tend to be an indoctrinator in his turn.

An obstacle to arriving at a clear conception and a clear definition of indoctrination is that the word is used in two different senses. It sometimes refers to a teaching technique whereby certain learning is imparted so that the pupil will retain it and be influenced by it for the remainder of his life. There are some things that the community wishes its children to learn in this fashion and when the technique is used on those things the indoctrination is condoned. At other times the term 'indoctrination' means the use of such a technique to persuade pupils to accept unquestioningly ideas which cannot be publicly agreed and which some of the community question. In those instances what is going on is not condoned by all, and when used in this sense the word 'indoctrination' is one of disapproval. It might lead to clearer thinking if we confined ourselves to the latter use and invented another word for the teaching process that succeeds in transmitting unshakable ideas of an acceptable nature.

Using the term in the second and narrower sense, indoctrination is a process whereby disputatious views or beliefs are taught in such a way that the learners do not recognise their disputatious nature and are conditioned not to give adequate consideration to the arguments against them or to contemplate the possibility of other views. To accomplish this there must be intention on the part of the teacher, efficient method and a successful outcome. Therefore, indoctrination is a word which we use to express our evaluation of a cluster of activities. R. S. Peters has said that education is a word we apply to a group of activities concerned with teaching and learning to signify our approval of them. He likens it to a *Good Housekeeping* seal of approval.[6] Indoctrination would seem to be a similar evaluative word applied to the same sort of activities to express disapproval. It is, however, more than a 'boo' word, because there are good grounds for the disapproval. Teaching, however well intended, which closes minds to cogent considerations and to valid arguments, as indoctrination does, ought not to have a place in any establishment which claims to give education.

Indoctrination and Religious Education

One way in which a teacher can place himself beyond the charge of being an indoctrinator is to confine his teaching to the first two types of content mentioned above – that is, to facts and to theories that command universal acceptance. Is it possible to do this in religious education and still deal adequately with the subject of religion? There certainly are some facts which can confidently be used, such as the dates of the lives of religious founders, the number of adherents of each faith, the length and names of the sacred books, and the dimensions and furnishings of religious buildings. There are also some generally agreed theories, mostly of moral ideals, which, by a process of interaction, are shared between a religion and the culture in which it operates. It is possible to detect a tendency in recent years for religious education to take refuge in this type of material and to become, in the lower forms, a study of sacred places, customs and objects, and, in the upper forms, a study of the history of religions or a discussion of moral issues. The question has to be raised of whether this is a study of religion or of its periphera.

   To teach about religion at a deeper level will involve beliefs, doctrines and commitments, which means dealing with content that is not only disputatious, but which is actually disputed by those outside the religion being studied, and it is then that religious education can become indoctrination unless the material is sensitively handled. One of the difficulties of doing this, especially if the teacher is a believer, is that religious doctrines do not look disputatious to the person who subscribes to them. The religious man claims that his ideas are true. They seem to be justified by some experience he has had, or because he thinks that they have been genuinely revealed to him, or because they are taught by some Church or some sacred writing whose authority he has accepted. Those who do not recognise them as truth he regards as ignorant or imperceptive or wickedly perverse. The arguments they advance against his beliefs do not seem cogent to him. Consequently he will be inclined to present doctrinal material in the same way as he presents verifiable facts, he will use expressions that presuppose its universal acceptance, and he will add to it sometimes an emotional warmth because of his keen commitment to it.

This will not look like indoctrination to him, but it will to those who do not share his beliefs. His reasons for those beliefs may seem conclusively valid to him, but they will not have the same compulsion for the outsider who has not had the experiences or made the commitment on which they are based. That is why religious education undertaken by a believer will be liable to be called indoctrination even by those sufficiently sympathetic to religion to consider that some beliefs ought, *in theory*, to be true, though still debatable. Those who reject all religious beliefs as erroneous will go further and say that it is worse than indoctrination and that it is the imparting of falsehoods by indoctrinatory methods. Furthermore, when religious education is aiming to attach pupils to a religion, to cause them to accept its beliefs as truths, then it is indoctrination to all who have not already accepted the doctrines.

Behind these differences of opinion is the question of whether or not religion is a form of knowledge. Is it possible to speak of 'religious knowledge' or only of 'religious belief'? On the one hand the logical positivists have argued that religious statements cannot be verified or falsified and so are meaningless. On this view there is nothing more to religion than belief statements of a very subjective kind. They are about non-rational commitments and so cannot be the subject of reasoned debate or of public education. On the other hand, Paul Hirst in his essay 'Liberal education and the nature of knowledge'[7] includes religion in his list of the forms of knowledge and Philip Phenix in *Realms of Meaning*[8] argued that religion is a valid 'overarching' way of understanding human experience. Between the two, some modern theologians, influenced by later Wittgensteinian ideas, seem concerned to establish that religious talk is valid within its own terms of reference and cannot be reduced to other forms of discourse or criticised by them.[9] The problem is to know what criteria can be applied to religious statements to test whether or not they are knowledge or subjective belief. If it could be established that religion is a form of knowledge with agreed criteria for testing its truth or falsehood religious education would be much easier to justify and less prone to condemnation as indoctrination. Meanwhile the 'multi-tiered doubt concerning religious statements'[10] means that acute difference of opinion is going to persist about how far religious education and religious indoctrination are inseparable. The debate continues.

Non-indoctrinatory Religious Education

If religious education is also to continue, those who teach it, while recognising that their subject cannot be placed beyond the charge of indoctrination in the eyes of everyone, will wish to make it as fair and acceptable as possible, and to respect the pupils' right to think for themselves and make up their own minds. To achieve this certain things have to be borne in mind and certain principles observed.

Firstly, the teacher will have to recognise, and keep in mind, the status of the material he is handling, distinguishing fact from belief. The latter cannot be taught as beyond question but as subject to discussion. In that discussion beliefs will have a different status for the believing pupils from what they will have for the unbelieving and the arguments for them will seem more cogent to believers. Classroom discussion of them cannot, therefore, lead to a unanimous agreement and it would be wrong to try and arrive at one. It is sufficient if, as a result of the talking, pupils respect beliefs even if they do not share them and realise that the people who hold them think they do so with good reason.

Secondly, the teacher will need to recognise the pluralist situation in which he is teaching. There are many beliefs and unbeliefs around and pupils have to be educated to live in that confusion. This gives the opportunity of examining the various beliefs to be found in a pluralist culture, the arguments for them and the

arguments against them. Such study can include consideration of
the criteria to be applied in assessing a belief, criteria such as
internal consistency, truth to experience, and such like.

Thirdly, when dealing with his own religion, if he has one, a
teacher needs to take particular care, recognising how his beliefs
may colour what he is doing. Consequently he will try to present
both the beliefs and the reasons for them on the one hand, and the
objections to them on the other, in an unemotional way. The
objections will be set out fully and fairly as well as alternative
beliefs. If he is a charismatic person who has built up an influential
relationship with his pupils he will beware of making undue use of
it to effect a response to his beliefs. Furthermore, when the beliefs,
the alternative beliefs, and the criteria by which both are to be
evaluated have been discussed he must be prepared to accept
whatever decision the pupils arrive at, provided it has been
seriously and sincerely made in the light of good evidence. There is
always the temptation that, having argued that his own faith is
defensible on rational grounds, and having had the arguments
rejected by pupils as invalid, the teacher will invoke other forms
of justification such as revelation or maintain that 'it all depends
on your faith'. Such sliding to another form of justification to make
up for the failure of the first is illogical and gives the impression
that the teacher is anxious to create faith 'regardless of the
evidence'. What it comes down to is that teachers of the subject
have to recognise that they are conducting religious education in a
school and not a church environment and to exercise the self-
discipline mentioned in Chapter 4 above, as well as face realistic-
ally the status of religion in the existing culture.

The foregoing is a counsel of perfection which, if achieved,
might lead to a cold and dull type of teaching. Teacher enthusiasm
and crankiness give warmth and excitement to lessons. If these
principles are rigidly applied it might not only rob the teaching of
that warmth but also give the impression that religion is a confused
matter of argument and counter-argument, which, by the very
nature of the subject being argued, cannot ever lead to conclu-
sions. The sense of adventure and commitment which is characteristic of religion could be obscured. By being taught that way the
subject might escape damnation as indoctrination by the uncom-
mitted, but it would instead incur the condemnation of the
religious that it misrepresents them and misses the point.

There is the possibility, moreover, that the attacks of secularists
on religious education have made teachers of it over-sensitive

about indoctrination. An entirely objective, non-indoctrinating teaching, excellent though it may be in theory, may not be invariably achievable in practice. A degree of indoctrination goes unchallenged in other subjects. For instance, the committed scientist who claims total objectivity is indoctrinating a commitment to objectivity, trying to impregnate a belief about a particular procedure for arriving at the truth. Children are subjected to multifarious indoctrinating pressures in school, through the media, through advertising and through arguments at home and with peers. It is part of their growing up to learn to resist these and to pick their way among them. The atheist, humanist and materialist groups do not scruple to urge their case and will counter any tendency of the religious education teacher to indoctrinate. It does not follow that religious education can unashamedly undertake indoctrination – that is the task of the evangelists of the religious bodies – but it does mean that the teacher can go about his task with a degree of robustness and not allow the present sensitiveness to indoctrination to push him into the obscureness of a complete uncriticalness about all beliefs and their justification, or to paralyse him into inactivity.

NOTES

1   P. Smart, 'The concept of indoctrination' (P. Smart, 1973, p. 37).
2   J. P. White, 'Indoctrination' (White, 1967, pp. 179ff.).
3   I. A. Snook (1972, p. 47).
4   Church of England Board of Education (1970, Appendix B).
5   White, *op. cit.*, p. 184.
6   R. S. Peters, *The Concept of Education*, p. 12.
7   P. H. Hirst, 'Liberal education and the nature of knowledge' (1972).
8   P. Phenix (1964).
9   E.g. I. M. Ramsey, Harvey Cox. Paul van Buren, etc.
10   Snook, *op. cit.*, p. 84.

Note on School Worship

The 1944 Act included two activities under the heading of religious education, an act of worship and learning in the classroom (and mentioned them in that order). The idea would appear to have been that what was learned in the lessons would be sincerely expressed in the worship in school assembly.

In the intervening years that daily act of worship has come increasingly under question for two main reasons. In the first place, little consideration was given to what worship implied in the school situation. Worship, it was assumed, was what went on in churches, so Christian liturgical worship was trimmed to appropriate size for the time available, and the daily school assembly included a mini church service. Such a ceremony presupposes certain beliefs in those participating. It is difficult sincerely to praise or pray to a God in which you do not believe, or about which you have doubts, and formal worship demands knowledge of its principles and experience of its practice for thorough-going involvement. Unless the school contains a high proportion of believers, both in pupils and staff, who are practised in traditional modes of worship, the religious observance it attempts is likely to be perfunctory and superficial. The increasingly secular outlook of society and the arrival in schools of immigrant children of diverse religious faiths has exacerbated the difficulties of producing genuine participation in school worship, which has become progressively problematic. In the second place, the redefining of religious education as a study of religions, with a view to understanding them rather than becoming attached to any one of them, has made a divide between the lessons and the worship. The classroom teaching is now, in many instances such that it does not lead to expression in worship (although what is done in worship may properly lead to discussion in the classroom).

This raises the question of whether school worship is any longer a necessary part of religious education. The answer to that question depends on how far it is essential to experience a religion and to take part in its worship in order to understand it. Moreover, even if we grant that such experience is needed, is school worship the best way of getting it? Religious education teachers are known to say that their pupils must be given some opportunity of taking part in worship in school because they will not encounter it elsewhere. Presumably they do not seek it elsewhere because it does not seem important to them. Will they, in such a state of mind, contribute anything to worship when they are forced to meet it in school assembly? If they need to experience worship, is it desirable that they should experience it in the low-temperature, do-it-yourself form, with many opting out or joining in reluctantly, that is sometimes characteristic of school worship? Or should some means be found of involving them in worship at its best and keenest?

To continue linking school worship with the lesson as two sides of religious education is causing confusion. It might lead to clarity to bear in mind that there are two distinct questions involved. The first is, how far is a school a religious community? Does it need to express its ethos and its apperceptions of meaning in regular ceremony? Or can it, like banks, factories, shops, offices, and institutions dealing with higher education, get on without it? That is a decision not for religious education specialists alone but for school governors, head teachers, the whole school staff, parents, and perhaps for the whole community. Should the answer to that question be 'no' there would still remain the further question of what ought to be taught about religion in schools to enable pupils to understand the world in which they live. Even if compulsory worship were discontinued in them, schools might still have to continue teaching about religion as a necessary ingredient of education.

Some modification of the existing situation seems needed. Many religious education teachers would welcome a distinction between religious education and school worship, and would like to see the legal provisions for the latter repealed, because the implication of the existing law is that the teaching is intended to be confessional. Furthermore, perhaps thought should be given to what form school 'worship' should take. Granted there is needed some way in which the school can express, as a whole, its ethos, its corporateness and its ideals, how can that be done in a way that is vivid and in which all pupils and staff can sincerely join? That expression might, or might not, include a religious element which could be called 'worship', according to the traditions of the school and the circumstances of the time. John Hull has discussed the possibility of what he calls 'secular assemblies' in his *School Worship: an Obituary* (S.C.M. Press, London 1974), and for a full discussion of the issues raised in this note the reader is referred to that book.

The Possibilities

9 The Concept of a Religiously Educated Person

The first two sections of this book have surveyed the history of religious education from the 1944 Education Act to the present time and discussed some of the problems that have arisen from it and which continue to impinge upon it. In the third section an attempt will be made to foresee what the subject will be like – or perhaps ought to be like – in the future. A number of questions have to be asked. Has the study of religion a necessary contribution to make to the education of a society in which religion has come to be regarded as a private matter? If so, can it be conducted in a way that will win it the support of everyone, parents, teachers of other subjects, educational administrators, and pupils, no matter what their beliefs or their estimate of the significance of religious beliefs? Is its purpose to teach about religion and religious practices, as an end in itself, or is it undertaken because such study will bring the students some further benefit or some more ultimate insight? How can it be taught to minimise the possibility of indoctrination or of misunderstanding of its language? All these questions lead to a more general one of what is religious education essentially trying to do at this point in history in the culture in which pupils and teachers are living?

As a prelude to considering these questions, it may help to try and arrive at a concept of a religiously educated person. What do we wish to emerge at the end of the religious education process about which it could be said, 'He has been properly educated about religion'? Moreover, there will be little point in getting a picture of that end-product unless we can describe the study and experiences that cause him to emerge and unless we can also justify teachers in the present educational system striving to produce him. In brief, we are considering the what, the how, and the why of a religiously educated man or woman.

The discussion is set in a particular context, namely in a secular and religiously pluralistic setting. It may well be that a religiously educated person in such a situation is different from what he would be in a faith situation. To illustrate this, consider what would have been thought to be a religiously educated man in Europe at the time when that continent could, with some degree of accuracy, call itself Christendom. In that situation there was only one religion, which was generally accepted as true, which permeated the culture and structured the civilisation of the time. All other religions were regarded as silly or dangerous superstitions. An educated man was expected to regard them as such, to disapprove of them, to disregard them, and when possible to persuade their adherents to abandon them for enlightenment, which meant to be converted to Christianity. This would seem to him a rational attitude because he, in common with everyone else around, was convinced of the truth of Christianity. That conviction would, furthermore, lead him to be a practising Christian, joining with the remainder of the community in its common worship, indulging in the accepted acts of personal devotion, and conforming to the ethic that Christian beliefs and doctrines imply. To do anything else would have seemed irrational, perverse and uneducated. Religious education would then consist of learning, approving, and practising the Christian beliefs and manners of life. Religious education and Christian conversion and nurture were synonymous. The same would be true, *mutatis mutandis*, of any other deeply held and totally accepted religious system. When such a situation exists religion is a comparatively simple thing and religious education a comparatively circumscribed activity. Teaching about the religion of the community is a normal part of the socialising process and schools do not need to do much about it because the cast of life and the pressure of social opinion is doing it for them; and their own ethos is so permeated with the religion that all the curriculum is contributing.

Needless to say our present culture is not like that. Those who deal with religious education consequently have a choice to make. They can either try to ignore the changed conditions, go on as before, and try to put the clock back and restore Christendom, or they can decide that it is necessary to react to the change and educate children to cope with the new religious situation that has arrived. Many seem to hanker for the former view, including a proportion of religious education teachers, whose practices still resemble those of their predecessors fifty years ago. Those who try to react to the altered environment have to ask themselves how their ideas of a religiously educated person have been modified by events and then decide what effect that modified view ought to have on their aims and practices.

What is the existing situation? It is that in Britain, owing to immigration and cultural change, we have a multiplicity of religions and of non-religious faiths. Some are Christians in the old church-going style. Others have a kind of residual Christianity or folk faith, the subterranean theology mentioned in Chapter 1 above. In addition there are those who think all religious beliefs are non-scientific and superstitious and that we should all adopt more rationalist ideologies; these are the Humanists, the scientific determinists, the Communists and the like. A large part of the population, one suspects, does not belong to any of these categories, being agnostic, thinking that there is no proof whether or not a supernatural God exists; he may or he may not, but the question is not normally relevant in a technological world where there are so many other things to think about. To these we must add, to make the mixture abundant in its rich variety, those immigrant faiths that have come among us, Muslim, Hindu, Sikh, Baha'i, and others, and those fringe cults that attract the young for a while, forms of Zen, the Jesus cults, scientology, followers of Sun Myung Moon, astrology, the occasional mysticism and others similar.

In such a pluralist setting the status of religion, the way in which people think about it, the esteem they accord it, and the function that it performs in society, are all different from what they are in a faith situation. When there are many religions and quasi-religions around no one of them emerges as the norm, the standard by which the others are to be judged. Consequently, there is no objective way of choosing between them. All are based on belief, not on demonstrably proven fact, and so, ideally, each is as good as the other, and, if you wish to be religious, it does not much matter which you choose. The ordering of society, and of the day-to-day life of individuals in it, is not centred round religion but decided on economic, financial, or hedonistic considerations. Religion becomes an optional extra, a hobby indulged in by those who have the taste for it, but having no imperative claim on attention. Large numbers appear to get along happily without much contact with it, and the claims of particular religions to truth and to be regulative of values and morals look empty and presumptuous. Religions are pushed out into the periphery of life, tolerated in all their forms with little attempt to distinguish between them. This evokes the question of whether religion has become so unimportant in its influence on society, and so much a matter of indifference to many, as to make difficult the justification of its study in schools.

There are, however, two things to notice in this connection. The first is that to a person who has adopted a religion its truth claims look true and imperative to him. He speaks of tenets of his religion not as beliefs or postulates but as truths. They provide the criteria by which he personally regulates his life and judges religions. To illustrate, Christian beliefs may not look like truths to a Humanist, a Maoist, or a Muslim, but they look like truths to a Christian. For him Christianity is the true religion and the others have at least a strong probability of falsehood. And the same would hold good of any other deeply held position.

The second thing to notice is that deeply held beliefs, of any sort, which are espoused as basic truths, affect radically the lives and characters of those who hold them. A Christian is what he is, and behaves as he does, frequently because he is a Christian. A Buddhist is what he is, and behaves as he does, frequently because he is a Buddhist. The word 'frequently' is included in those statements because one recognises that there are other influences besides religion forming life styles, but the argument is that a sincerely held belief, or set of beliefs, is likely to have a powerful formative effect. Moreover, everyone has some sort of basic beliefs, albeit not always clearly and consciously defined, some assumptions or working hypotheses, which are contributing to the formation of character and choice of actions. In some cases these beliefs will be religious, in others they may be scientific, personal, hedonistic, humanistic, political, or some other. If we are to understand people and what makes them tick we need to know something about the effects of belief in general and of the beliefs of individuals in particular. Here is a basic source of human motivation. It may be diverse and it may be such that we do not feel able to judge between its diverse forms, but some intelligence about it would seem necessary if we are to understand the people around us and the culture they are creating. Here is one justification for the study of religions, even though it may have to be set in the wider context of the study of belief systems generally, including those that would not wish to be described as religious.

What would it mean to be educated about religion in the pluralistic situation described above? Merely to have learned about one religion, and to regard others, which are sincerely held over wide areas, as unworthy of serious attention, would seem insufficient. Education involves helping pupils to cope with the environment in which they live and in a pluralistic situation that means helping them to cope with religions and belief systems other than their own. Perhaps we can move towards answering the question if we consider what education in general aims to do. What is an educated man in any field? He is not necessarily a man filled to the ears with knowledge. It has sometimes been thought that an educated man is a walking encyclopaedia. The writer has memories, in his youth, of having his education called in question because he could not immediately produce a piece of information such as how high is St Paul's Cathedral, or how deep is the Atlantic Ocean at its deepest part, or how many pigeons can stand comfortably on the hat of Nelson's statue in Trafalgar Square, or some similarly unimportant piece of learning. But an educated man is more than a well-stuffed memory. Certainly he will have some knowledge and he will have the technique to discover more when it is needed. He will know where and how to look for information. His distinguishing feature, however, is that he will know how to use the knowledge when it has been acquired and be discriminating and intelligent about it.

If we apply the foregoing to religion there would seem to be four characteristics of a religiously educated person.

(a)   He will have acquired certain information about religion. One would hardly call him educated if he were entirely ignorant about it. He will not know everything, but he will know enough to be able to think about the subject, and he will know where to acquire further knowledge when he needs it.

(b)   He will have some appreciation of the function of religion in the lives of individuals and in the ordering of society. That is, he will have an understanding of why human beings have acquired and systematised beliefs, forming religions and Churches and sects, and of what those organised bodies contribute to social life and to culture.

(c)   He will be able to make informed and discriminating decisions, based on conscious criteria, about religious beliefs and religious practices. He will know what questions have to be asked about them and the basis on which they can be compared and judged. Therefore when he approves or disapproves of some religious manifestation

he will be able to give reasons for his approval or disapproval.

(d)   He will be conscious of what he himself believes, the
reasons for those beliefs, and their effect on his choices and
actions. This will imply knowing what he does not believe – what religious teachings he rejects – his reasons for
this disbelief and the practical effect of his doubting. Some
may believe a good deal more than others, and some may
believe very little, but all, if they are educated in the
religious field, ought to know where they stand and why
they stand there.

If these are the true characteristics of a religiously educated
person, his chief mark will be a capacity to understand and to
judge critically, rather than an abundance of knowledge about, or
an inclination to accept, beliefs. It is not suggested that an
educated response precludes the sincere and committed adoption
of any belief provided that seems the proper course to the pupil; it
will demand that such a decision be genuine, conscious, informed
and based on reasoned consideration of what is involved.

More teachers of the subject than formerly are seeing their task
in that light, but it is not always easy for them to do so. Many have
chosen to teach the subject in the first place because they have a
religious commitment which is likely to affect how they regard
religious education. For them, their religion is the true one and
provides the criteria on which these supposedly objective assessments of religious beliefs and practices are to be made. They may
not be openly trying to convert pupils to their way of thinking, but
it is hard for them to avoid the wish that they could or the hope that
they will. While few have the attitude of the teacher who when one
of her class enquired about a Buddhist belief replied, 'Some
people have that erroneous opinion', there can often be an ambivalence in their attitude to their work. A similar ambivalence is
frequently found in writings about religious education, which,
while setting out a theory of education as making students objectively intelligent about what is being studied, have the underlying
assumption that a certain set of religious beliefs are the ones which
must inevitably be found to be true.[1]

So much for the theory of the type of individual that religious
education in a pluralistic society should be trying to produce. We
have now to consider how such discerning animals are made. The
object is not to describe a few straightforward activities which, if
set in process will cause religiously educated pupils to pop up in all

corners of the classroom. There are no such tricks, and educating about religion is a long-term activity which will meet with varying success according to the responsiveness and sensitivity of the pupils. Instead there are certain basic areas of activity which can be tried. It will mean more than telling pupils facts about religions, acquainting them with the stories and literature of religions and asking them to join in some elementary devotional exercises in school assembly. The business is more complex than that, and there are six areas of activity to be provided.

Firstly, early on in the infant and junior school in the main, though continuing throughout school life and beyond, there are certain sensitivities to be provoked and developed. There is no call to describe them fully here since they are set out in Chapter 3 above (see pages 39–41).

Secondly, pupils can be helped to understand that religion is a particular way of thinking which may be valid within its own terms of reference, with its own way of setting out its thoughts and its own vocabulary. This means teaching about the language of religion which is discussed in Chapter 6 above (see pages 70–87).

The third activity is helping pupils investigate the way in which beliefs affect actions, how a person's religion, if sincerely applied, makes him tend to behave in a particular way. A good deal of this is being done by studies of heroes and saints and religiously motivated modern figures, showing how they are sustained by their faith and driven on by it to attempt the unusual and the difficult. This goes some way towards showing the connection between belief and practice, but confining the study to outstanding and exceptional figures has the side-effect of suggesting that only the exceptional are religiously motivated and that religious impulses do not affect ordinary people. It puts religious motivation in a kind of Valhalla. It might be more helpful if, in addition, opportunity were provided for older pupils to meet religious people of various sorts who would be prepared to state simply and to discuss what they personally believe and how they think their beliefs affect their attitudes and their actions. When this has been tried teachers have found that it has evoked pupils' interest, extended their insights, and sometimes significantly modified their attitude to religion. The problem is to find the right people to do it. It would help if religious bodies were prepared to set up in each district a panel of men and women who would be prepared to talk about their religion honestly and unaggressively, and without attempting to sell their opinions. They would need to be carefully chosen and perhaps volunteers should be automatically excluded.

Fourthly, provision has to be made to call attention to the affective element in religions. Besides having a set of intellectual propositions a religion has an emotional content which is as important a part of its motivation as its credal statements. A religious man not only believes and thinks, he also feels. The feeling is most obvious and intense at moments of mystic experience and times of prayer and worship. Full education about a religion, therefore, involves recognition and understanding of the feelings behind its mystic practices and its public worship. When dealing with this, religious education has more in common with music than with mathematics. One could hardly be thought to be musically educated if one knew the dates of all the great composers' lives, the keys and opus numbers of all their symphonies, but was not aware of the thrill that can come from hearing those symphonies being played. Similarly one is not really educated about religion if one knows all the creeds in creation and the moral injunctions of each ideology but knows nothing of the feelings that go with the creeds and injunctions and with the practice of worship.

Not a great deal of thought has been given, until very recently, about how this aspect of religion should be treated in education. It has usually been assumed that it was necessary to cause pupils to experience such feelings by giving them religious experiences in the school assembly. This increasingly seems to have the taint of indoctrination and in practice has often led to formality, scepticism and boredom. Something else might be more effective and two possibilities suggest themselves. In the first place, religious feelings are ordinary human feelings expressed or interpreted in the light of religious beliefs. If pupils can be helped to recognise that the 'religious emotions' are akin to emotions that they themselves frequently experience, but expressed in a manner that seems appropriate to believers, they may find a degree of sympathy with them. It would involve the teacher in some such teaching as the following: Let us look at a body of religious people at prayer, 'confessing their sins', and try to understand how they are feeling. Those who are being sincere, and not merely going through the motions, are feeling guilty and contrite. Recall the occasions when in your own life, quite apart from religion, you have had similar feelings, when you have felt guilty at having hurt someone, or acted in a way that aroused a bad conscience. That is how those folk are feeling, and they are trying to cope with the unpleasant emotion by reference to their religious beliefs which helps them to come to terms with the tensions the emotion causes. Similarly, let us look at a body of religious people who are indulging in an act of praise and try to understand how they are feeling. They are glad and happy, so call to mind occasions when you felt like that. Recall how you expressed that happiness in singing, jumping for joy, thanking your parents and other appropriate ways. Those people are doing that, but their mode of expressing joy is conditioned by their beliefs, so that they do not jump or throw their hats in the air, but use the forms of expression that are customary in their church or synagogue or mosque or temple. They do it by singing 'psalms and hymns and spiritual songs'[2] or, as they might say, by 'making melody in their hearts unto the Lord',[3] or by praising Allah, say. Once the basic human feelings involved in religious experience are recognised, it is much easier to sympathise with it, to see the cause of religious emotion, to perceive how it is expressed, and to be tolerant and discerning about it.

The other thing that might help is the study of art, both religious and otherwise. The artist, be he painter, poet, musician, sculptor or other, is trying to convey the emotions that arise from his experience of perception. In times of faith this is influenced by the prevailing belief and produces what is (perhaps wrongly) called 'religious art'. In secular ages the obvious religious reference may be lacking and the affective reaction, though basically the same, expressed in other terms. More time in the religious education lesson might profitably be given to the study and enjoyment of art forms of all kinds, followed by the discussion of how the perceptions and feelings to which they draw our attention are found, differently expressed, in religious practices.

These are two methods by which it might be possible to produce discernment about 'religious feelings' without necessarily trying to induce the feelings themselves. At the same time, some pupils might well find that they could sincerely join in the expression of emotions in a religious form, though an educational approach would neither forbid nor encourage (or even hope for) that result.

The fifth activity in producing a religiously educated person is the imparting of an understanding of how most religions have a theory of revelation and of how some special knowledge has been vouchsafed to the adherents by prophecy or incarnation or avatar. This has been discussed in Chapter 5 above (pages 64–9) and need not be further dealt with here.

Finally, the sixth activity is learning facts about religion. It has been left till last because it is the most commonplace, and the one that makes up the whole programme of some teachers. The problem about it is that there are now so many facts to be taught. When religious education was concerned only with Christianity there was plenty to do with the whole of the Bible, Church History, examples of Christian lives, Church practices, Church worship, private devotions and Christian ethics to be included. Now that it has also to include many religions, fringe religions and non-religious 'life stances', the task is impossible. How can a teacher with one or two lessons a week, give or take a homework, possibly get it all into limited heads in the limited time at his disposal? What does he concentrate on? Which of it is vitally important? The problem is eased somewhat if the imparting of facts about religions is not regarded as an end in itself, but as a means to other educational ends. If fundamentally religious education is trying to convey understandings about religion,[4] abilities to think about it such as are entailed in the five activities previously mentioned, almost any of the mass of information available can be used to that purpose. Instead of looking at it as a mound of facts to be systematically transmitted, perhaps it should be regarded as a quarrying ground from which to excavate a sufficient number of examples to illustrate the principles involved in understanding. In this respect it can be compared with what is done in the teaching of mathematics. The teacher of arithmetic shows his pupils how to add. He does not then require them to do all the addition sums there are, for that would take a lifetime and more. Instead he provides sufficient examples to ensure that his pupils understand and can practise addition, and then he goes on to teach subtraction and provides an adequate number of examples of that. Similarly, if religious education is the imparting of skills, then the facts can be used to provide examples on which to practise those skills. It is not necessary to impart every fact about every religion, but sufficient to allow the learners to grasp and think about the principles. Nor need every teacher make use of the same set of facts. A Christian teacher could use the facts of his faith and a Muslim teacher the facts of his faith to lead to identical understandings.

There will, of course, be a modicum of facts to be taught in order to give a balanced view of a religion and pupils probably need to know more facts about the religions they are likely to meet in their own neighbourhood than about those in remote parts that they are unlikely frequently to encounter. Selection of content may have to vary from place to place. One may have to include more facts about Islam when teaching in Bradford or Baghdad than one would in Barnstaple or Ballachulish. This will in general mean that in Britain an emphasis will be placed on the teaching of facts about Christianity, with Humanism a good second. The purpose of teaching facts, however, is not simply to inform, for there is more to being educated about religion than knowing facts. Acquiring facts is but a prelude to being intelligent about them and the ultimate aim of the exercise in a pluralist world is to give the pupils the skills to be so intelligent.

NOTES

1 My own book *Changing Aims in Religious Education* (1966) has, probably rightly, been charged with this ambivalence. I hope this writing may be adjudged more consistently objective.
2 Ephesians 5, 19.
3 Ibid.
4 For an attempt to define the understandings necessary to grasp the essentials of a religion see Schools Council Occasional Bulletin, *A Groundplan for the Study of Religion* (1977).

10 Future Justification, Shape and Content

Having looked at the history of religious education since 1944, having considered some of the problems that beset it at the present, and having tried to envisage its end product in the form of a religiously educated person, perhaps consideration should now be given to the possible form of the subject in the future and the contribution it can make to the process of educating pupils to meet the demands of living at the end of the twentieth century. If that contribution is to be worthwhile the subject needs to acquire both shape and justification.

The Need for Shape and Justification

The Schools Council document, *Groundplan for the Study of Religion*[1] points out that 'In the thirty years since the Education Act, the subject has lost its well-defined appearance. Its definite outlines have become blurred, its content less concise, and its purpose less plain.' This present indecision about its aims and its content is the result of two influences. Firstly, the different types of religious education which have been fashionable since 1944, the confessional, the neo-confessional, the implicit and the explicit, are all being practised, so that teachers are by no means agreed about their aims. Some teachers see their task as giving pupils a belief in God, others as attaching them to some form of Christianity as the religion that has provided the shaping impetus of existing Western culture and morals. There are those who wish their pupils to have the support of a religion, but, recognising that a person's belief is conditioned by cultural, psychological and experiential factors, are tolerant about which faith is chosen, while some of their colleagues are hoping for a specific commitment (usually their own). Others hope their teaching will lead children to have a sensitive approach to life, and to understand and face some of the deeper philosophical problems that experience raises, but would regard it as bordering on indoctrination to try to incline pupils to come to terms with that sensitivity or to solve those problems by recourse to a set of typical beliefs. They are content to provoke thought about the issues with which religions and life stances deal, while leaving the individual student to respond to them in the way that seems appropriate to his good sense and culture. Such teachers are the heirs of the Loukesian 'implicit religious approach' of the 1960s. The chief fashion of the last decade, however, has been to follow the 'explicit religion approach' and to think of the subject as the objective study of religions in the hope that the pupils will sympathetically understand them, but without necessarily being affected by them in any other way. With these several and widely differing aims being attempted – and hotly debated – the subject has the appearance of conflict and incoherence.

Secondly, the widening of the subject from the study of Christianity to the discussion of the religious aspects of social and personal problems had led to its extending itself across the curriculum and overlapping with other lessons that were not previously regarded as religious. Some of what is now practised as religious education could also be called social education or moral education or aesthetic appreciation. There is, for instance, a marked similarity between books for the study of English literature and some of those that are provided for the study of religious issues. Teachers are occasionally asked to explain in what way their lesson content is contributing to education in religion, and how it differs from social studies or humanities studies or cultural education. By this extension of its borders religious education has become diffuse and ill-defined and a new definition of the subject seems needed to give it coherence and shape.

The matter of the subject's justification is equally pressing, since its status as an essential part of education is both asserted and denied within the educational system itself and without. Unlike some subjects (for example, mathematics) which are accepted by pupils, teachers, school governors, administrators, governments, and men and women of all persuasions as an indispensible ingredient of education, religious education is at present forced to make its case to those who suspect that it no longer has anything to offer. Among these are certain pupils who show by their indifference to the study, and occasionally their overt scorn of it, that they would not feel over-deprived if it disappeared. Their attitudes range from a suspicion of irrelevance, as in the case of the boy who asked, 'What is the use of religious education unless you are going to be a Vicar?', to a deep antipathy to the subject matter. Furthermore, there are the reservations of teachers of other subjects. Some of them value the subject and are supportive of their religious education colleagues, but there can be few of the latter of long service who have not been the recipients of comments, that are apparently semi-humorous but of serious underlying intent, which suggest that their subject is footling and possibly mislead-ing. There are, in addition, instances of other subjects being taught in such a way as to imply that they have an absolute truth which negates religious ideas and that anything taught in the religious education lesson must be patently incredible. Nor can it be assumed that all head teachers are equally enthusiastic about the educational value of teaching about religion. Some are, but the Religious Education Council's submission to the Secretary of State in 1980 stated that 25% of comprehensive schools provide no religious education and that a great number of secondary schools omit it after the third year. Presumably decisions on what is or what is not included in the curriculum are mainly influenced by the head's opinion and so these figures suggest that not all heads regard religious education as imperative. Outside the school there are parents who sometimes object to religious teaching and with-draw their children, or, more likely, do not withdraw their children and grumble. In addition, there are the pressure groups some of which want the subject changed and others of which want it abolished. Among the former are the religious groups who wish their views to be presented more aggressively, perhaps more dogmatically, and who complain that much of what now passes for religious education is too liberally tolerant and gives pupils a freedom of choice which they are not mature enough safely to exercise. The British Humanist Association takes the contrary view that the subject is not liberal enough and should be extended to include all life-stances, and the hard line Humanists take the line that all teaching of religion in schools is indoctrinatory in intent and should be abolished. For instance, the *Free Thinker* in its December 1980 issue, was liberal with its free thoughts in an article entitled 'Religious Education is Dying on its Feet' in which it quoted Nicholas Walter to the effect that 'The great majority of humanists want not any kind of revival of the present system of religious education but its replacement by a completely different system of genuine education about religion, philosophy and morality.'

The foregoing catalogue of dissent must not obscure the support that the subject has, not only from the religious bodies, but also from parents, heads, and other teachers, from many who think seriously and dispassionately about education and about the ethos of society and from a large section of the public that has a gut feeling that religion ought to be included in education without being able to say explicitly why or to define exactly what they hope for it or expect it to do for the young.

The result is that at present religious education is a school activity which arouses wide differences of opinion and sometimes acute dispute. Its educational credentials are not agreed, its precise contribution to the curriculum unclear, and its support often a matter of hunch and undefined feeling, rather than of logical, publicly defensible argument. The question to be faced is whether it can be redefined and restructured in such a way as will give it both shape and justification. The continuance of religious education as a regular and general ingredient in the curriculum may depend on discovering a conception of it which all who teach it can agree upon and conscientiously accept, which will give it unity and direction, and which will make clear its distinctive contribution to children's learning. Such a view might, moreover, lead to it being accepted by all administrators and school heads as an indisputable element in the curriculum, to its being supported by those who teach other subjects, whatever their personal belief, as feeding in to what they themselves are teaching, to its being welcomed by parents, to its being recognised by pupils as worthy of their attention (as far as the frailties of youthful volatility will permit), and to its being understood as desirable by all members of the public whatever religion or life-stance they accept or reject. Such a utopian conception of the subject may be difficult in the existing situation, but without it religious study in schools will not remain a part of the core curriculum but will be in danger of 'dying on its feet' or in being relegated to a peripheral activity, tolerated as an option for those who happen to have the taste for it.

A New Rationale?

For religious education to be universally accepted in the way envisaged above it would have to be attempting something that everyone agrees is enlightening and enlarging pupils' minds and outlooks, which no one can complain is misleading or misinforming them, and which will relate to some of the accepted disciplines in the academic world. In practice, it will have to use material which is thought worthwhile in the present culture and with which pupils can feel able to respond with warmth and interest, and in its outcome it will need to convey some knowledge or insight which will enable them to understand better other people's belief systems and clarify their own beliefs. It is possible that none of the conceptions of the subject held at present meet those specifications. An examination of the two ideas that have mainly influenced recent Agreed Syllabuses, such as those of Birmingham, Cheshire, Avon and Hampshire, shows that neither quite achieves what is needed.

One of those ideas is that religious education is necessary for an understanding of the culture in which we live. That culture, it is said, is deeply infused with religious ideas and values and cannot be deeply appreciated apart from them. Such a view was expressed by Lord Blake in a debate about religious education in the House of Lords in May 1977.

> It is my view that education that excludes religion altogether is surely not education. If children are taught nothing about one of the greatest forces which have shaped the world they live in, and one of the aspects of human culture which has affected people in one form or another for thousands of years, they are missing something profoundly important.[2]

There is much truth in this, but the religious influence in our culture has diminished in this century and other forces, such as economics, political theory, liberal hedonism and aggressive self-interest, are shaping our culture to a greater extent than religious ideals. Children probably still need to know what contribution religion is making, but that contribution may not be extensive enough to invoke it as a justification for a completely separate school subject, since it could adequately be covered under the heading of history or of social studies.

The other way in which the subject is presently justified is to say that it is a necessary study of an important aspect of human experience. The argument is that religious experience is likely to strike everyone, even though all do not recognise it, that it has a considerable effect on individuals and on their relationships, and that religious education should attempt to convey some understanding of it. Mary Warnock, in her book, *The Way Ahead*, expresses it in these words:

> I am convinced that RE ought to be taught in all schools but that it ought to be taught by people who like and believe in religion and who know something about it first hand. It is perfectly possible for such people to give an acquaintance with the Bible and the Prayer Book, and a sense of what a powerful force religion can be both historically and as a source of aesthetic inspiration. Without some such teaching children are actually deprived of understanding a part of the world they live in. Every school ought to provide this kind of teaching, just as much as it ought to provide teaching of history or of literature.[3]

Leaving aside the implied restriction of religious education to 'acquaintance with the Bible and the Prayer Book', one can agree with this while still questioning whether it provides a wide enough basis for a universally acceptable justification for a separate school subject, on the grounds that it assumes a validity for religious experience that not all admit. There are those who deny the existence of experience that can properly be called 'religious', and who think that those who claim to have had a religious experience are talking about something that might better be described in psychological and sociological terms.

None the less, the study of belief experiences and their effect may have a place in education, provided that it is set in a wider context. The Agreed Syllabuses of the late 1970s have tended to set it in the narrow context of an implicit and phenomenological study of religions. This has given shape and clear borderlines to the subject by making it a detached study of religious people and their practices and beliefs. At first glance this phenomenological approach has much to commend it. By studying many religions in an objective way, without trying to attach the learner to any one of them, it evades the suspicion of indoctrination; it links up with the academic study of theology, history and sociology; it has the educational advantage of starting not with abstract beliefs but with religious practices, religious objects and religious places, in which, it is claimed, pupils find a keen interest; and it deals with an important aspect of human experience.

On closer inspection some of these claims look less cogent. Does an external study of the actions and objects of religious behaviour lead to a genuine appreciation of the motives that prompt that behaviour, or does an understanding of what religion means require some more personal involvement? Can younger children approach the work with the dispassion that phenomenological study needs? Will they, if they are mentally alert, rather be deciding that they agree or disagree with the religious people whose behaviour they are considering, and if they have not grasped the motivation behind the ceremonies are they not likely to dismiss them as unworthy of further thought, as the peculiar way in which some folk choose inexplicably to behave? If so, the study could lead to superficial rejection rather than the desired sympathetic insight. Moreover, is the study as evocative of pupil interest as is claimed? It may arouse the curiosity of the younger ones, who are still examining the world with eager interest and prepared to be delighted, and not over critical, of what they find. Older ones, however, may be more blasé and ask what is the point of devoting time to the study of religious manifestations when there are other aspects of human experience that they find more attractive and urgent. There is evidence that secondary school pupils take this line, and they may well be influenced by the reaction to this type of teaching mentioned previously in this paragraph. But perhaps the chief weakness of the phenomenological approach, as a justifiable mode of religious education, is its claim to be dealing with a significant aspect of human experience. The claim may well be true, but is its truth recognised by sufficient people for religious education to be accepted by all as worthy of school time? Is religion seen as sufficiently worth-while by contemporary men and women to compete successfully for curriculum space? Or is it regarded as a private matter, an optional hobby for the few? It may look worth-while to professional theologians, to religious education teachers, and to religiously minded bodies and individuals, but does it seem so to the majority of parents, tax payers, other teachers and students? Do pupils throughout their school career rate religions highly enough, and find them intriguing enough to be ready to give their attention to prolonged serious study of them? If the answer to those questions is 'yes', then phenomenological religious education is justified. But if the answer is 'no', even though religion may be a significant human experience, then religious education so conducted will not receive the widespread support that it needs at present for its justification.

If the aims of religious education currently put forward do not permit universal acceptance of it, what conception of it is likely to be more successful? Disagreement about the status and credibility of religion renders it impossible to achieve the necessary consensus as long as we confine the subject to the study of religion or religions. Consequently, the justification of religious education may have to be found outside religion altogether. If it cannot be argued that religious education should be taught because religion is true or popular or useful or cultural, then in order to justify it one has to show that it, and it alone, provides some other social understanding or personal knowledge that pupils need. That involves putting it in a wider educational context so that it is contributing, along with other learning, to the provision of a universal insight which all need to acquire in order to understand what life is about. Then it would be accepted as valid by all.

It can be argued that the 1944 Act intended the subject to serve a deeper purpose than to promote a study of religion, but that in the ecclesiastical and theological discussion that was necessary for the production of Agreed Syllabuses this further objective became obscured. The White Paper that preceded the Act stated that the subject 'should be given a more definite place in the life and work of the schools . . . to revive spiritual and personal values in our society and in our national tradition'.[4] That seems to have been lost sight of in the intervening years, during which a self-conscious and self-absorbed religious education has become increasingly beset with intractible problems, but it has come to light again in recent official publications. The Green Paper of 1977 included in its list of the aims of education: 'to instil a respect for moral values, for other people, and for self, and tolerance of other races, religions and ways of life', and 'to teach children about human achievements and aspirations in art and science and in religion'.[5] The document *A Framework for the School Curriculum* (1980) stated that 'it is right . . . for religious education to be linked with the wider consideration of personal and social values'.[6] The later publication *The School Curriculum* (1981) echoes this:

> The place of religious education in the curriculum and its unique statutory position accord with a widely shared view that the subject has a distinctive contribution to make to a pupil's school education . . . It forms part of the curriculum's concern with personal and social values, and can help pupils understand the religious and cultural diversity of contemporary society.[7]

There has, furthermore, been an awareness of the need for education to give to learners not only knowledge but a vision of the overall purpose of life and a consciousness of what values are underlying their life styles. For instance G. W. Allport has described the marks of maturity as:

> First a variety of interests which concern themselves with ideals, objects and values . . . Second, the ability to objectify oneself, to be effective and insightful about one's own life . . . Finally some unifying philosophy of life, not necessarily religious in type, nor articulated in words, nor entirely complete. But without the direction and coherence supplied by some dominant pattern, any life seems fragmented and aimless.[8]

Mary Warnock points out how human needs are ultimately caused by the values a person holds.

> Whenever someone says he needs something, it is always proper to ask him what he needs it for, and his answer will specify something that he values.[9]

J. P. White considers that a school leaver should, among other things, understand 'the wide range of possible ways of life open to him and to others, and to have begun to assess, to some extent, these different ways, so as to decide which he will follow'.[10] This implies a search for life ideals, or for a unifying principle which would 'connect the many parts of his disconnected existence into some kind of harmony'. He concludes:

> Since in order to integrate their life in the present sense, students will have to understand different ways of life as well as different isolable activities, some kind of religious education is essential at this point.[11]

If we place religious education in this context, it becomes part of the search of growing human beings for integration and for consciously held, adequate, directive values. The theory behind it is that all values and value systems depend on the assumption of certain axia or certain beliefs about the nature of reality and of man. These beliefs and the value systems that are derived from them affect the ways men live and the communities that they strive to create. For instance, the Russian Revolution and the Nazi and Fascist movements were motivated by distinct beliefs about the nature of man and his relationship to his fellows and his environment. In a pluralist world these beliefs take a religious form for

some and a secular form for others, and study of them in schools
has to include both forms, probably as part of one subject.
Religion will be an important part of the content of the study
because of its historical influence on the formation of existing
values, and because that influence is still powerful, as recent
events in Northern Ireland and Iran have shown. At the same time
it will take its place alongside, and relate to, a study of other belief
systems from which honest and intelligent people have derived
their values. Thus although this conception of the subject has
affinity with the Loukesian 'implicit religious' education, which
looked at experience to discover the meaning and values behind it,
there is a difference in that it goes beyond a Christian, or even a
specifically religious, framework.

A New Structure?

If it be granted that religious education in the future will be an
integral part of a wider study of human aspirations and values,
there arises the question of how religions would be dealt with in
the syllabuses and in the actual teaching in order to convey the
sought insights. Ideally it should try to meet the following requirements. It should:

1 relate to the understanding of the pupils at the various stages
   of their development;
2 deal with matters that the pupils feel are relevant and important to their lives (and consequently interesting);
3 enable pupils to understand better the world in which they
   have to live and the people in it;
4 acquaint them with the ideals and aspirations of men and
   women in their search for meaning and value;
5 provide them with information about some of the religions
   and belief constructions (or life-stances) that have shaped
   surviving cultures and what their contribution to those cultures has been;
6 deal with those belief systems in a way that does justice to
   them and is acceptable to their followers;
7 increase pupils' powers of discrimination and ability to think
   about belief systems and their influence on individual and
   community values;
8 enable them to move towards coming to terms with their own

life problems by means of a coherent and conscious set of beliefs.

To meet these specifications the syllabus would include the following sections. The first would be the cultivation of the sensitivities described in Chapter 3, leading to a realisation that they raise questions such as, 'Why is anything here?' 'How do I relate to the people and the world around me?', 'How ought I to behave?', 'What is my significance as a person?', and leading also to a recognition of the emotions of awe, fear, wonder, joy, and so on that are attendant upon the asking and answering of those questions. Secondly, there would be the consideration of how answers to those questions have been given in the past, either by people searching earnestly for them or feeling that the answers have been disclosed to them, and of how, by ceremonies and stories, religions have tried to express and to cope with the emotions that sensitive questioning evokes. Thirdly, the syllabus would deal with the manner in which answers to the questions have led individuals to formulate ideals and aspirations, and to hold certain things as valuable and worth seeking, and to choose their actions and their life-styles in the light of those ideals. This would include learning about how the ideals have also been expressed in ceremony and in story and about how the life-styles have been defined in sets of commandments and moral injunctions. Finally study would be undertaken of how all this response to experience, apprehension of reality, and formation of value systems and life-styles have been formalised and perpetuated in religions.

It is not suggested that those four sections should be dealt with sequentially in the actual teaching. They form the ingredients of the subject, but the order in which they are presented would be modified to meet the interest and capabilities of the pupils at the different stages of their development. In the primary school teachers would be concerned with developing the basic sensitivities of wonder, change and relationship, and the simpler questions that emerge, such as:

What am I like?

How do I treat other people?

What decisions do folk make about how they spend their time and live their lives?

How do those decisions affect all of us?

At this level the subject would deal with simple observation of the nature of things that children can see around them and of how people make choices, which has the advantage of beginning with pupils' experience. They can examine their own physical structure and abilities, look at the qualities and behaviour of objects in the created world, and notice that people have trades and hobbies and customs that they have, to an extent, chosen. They can discuss those choices, such as why has X chosen to be a milkman, or a policeman, or a school teacher, and how does his choice affect him and us in a practical way. This may not, at casual glance, seem closely connected with the beliefs, mystic experiences and devotional practices of religions, but it is the preliminary to considering the grounds on which people make decisions, which will, in the end, lead to an appreciation of how a man's mystical intuitions of reality (his religion or his life-stance) have inclined him to commitments which can seem deep and imperative and which give direction to his choices and decisions.

That next step belongs to the middle years of schooling when harder questions have to be faced, such as:

In what ways do men and women come to a sense of meaning in experience and use their lives in a satisfying, and perhaps significant, way?

How have they tried to explain the meaning they have found and to justify the ways of life they have chosen?

In practice this means looking at the decisions that groups of people have made and their reasons for making them. It includes learning about the universal myths of search and about the lives of seers and prophets and religious innovators, who have tried to pass on to others the intimations of (or revelations of) reality that have come to them. This is the theme of much of the sacred literature of religions, suitable portions of which may be read at this stage. Furthermore, insights of reality are not expressed only by philosophical pronouncements and theological doctrines, but also in story, art, music, poetry, dance, drama, in religious ceremonies, festivals and sacraments. An examination of how religious ideas and emotions are so expressed will be included in the curriculum, and this probably means providing opportunity for pupils to indulge in these things, in so far as their genuine beliefs will permit, in order that they know how they feel from the inside. If such teaching activities produce sympathy with spiritual search, they will be helping the pupils to become aware of their own intuitions and enquiries and half-conscious commitments, with the result that they will be starting to work out their own sincere religion or life-stance.

If the preceding activities have been organised in the infant and junior schools, pupils may have been led to appreciate what religion is about, what influence it has on the formation of individual and communal life-styles, and from this may come an interest in further study because they see its relevance to an understanding of the effect of the multi-beliefs they encounter in a pluralistic world. The secondary school would, therefore, be concerned with a study of the way in which men and women of like commitment join together to form organised religions, with their creeds and commandments and forms of worship, and find within that organisation both clarification and reinforcement of their personal commitments. The questions being answered at this stage are:

> What decisions are involved when individuals group together for the promotion of common interest and mutual edification? What have belief systems to say about the decisions we all have to make? How do they help us:
>
> (i)   to understand and develop ourselves? (*the personal aspect of religion*)
> (ii)   to decide how to make ourselves useful? (*the communal aspect of religion*)
> (iii) to decide how to treat others? (*the moral aspect of religion*)
> (iv)   to decide about the meaning and significance, if any, of the totality of experience? (*the doctrinal aspect of religion*)

This would be a more structured study of religions, strongly resembling the type of religious education that has been customary in the past. It would, however, go beyond information-giving. Conducted on comparative lines, it would aim to show pupils that, although all religions are concerned with similar basic questions, the answers they give, the form of the doctrines they propound, the content of the ceremonies they provide, and the type of stories they employ as myths are determined by the cultures from which they spring; and there would be posed perpetually the problem of what effect is our existing culture having on the way in which we express our intimations of reality and on what we hold to be of value. At this stage, too, religions would have to be related to the other aspects of a subject that tries to deal with the formation and influence of human values, namely those non-religious value systems by which secular men organise themselves, thereby setting specific religious education into the wider educational context described on pages 133–5 above.

These are the general outlines of a structure for religious education, so that it would progress from a simple examination of self and surroundings, through the study of personal and social decisions, to a contemplation of some of the deepest problems of practical conduct and philosophical understanding, and the manner in which specific religions and other belief systems attempt to solve those problems. To describe the content of the subject in this sequential way is, to an extent, misleading because the conduct of religious education cannot be linear. It is dealing with questions that are asked continually at all ages of life, and so it is not a case of 'learning this and then going on to that'. The ideas behind the 'this' recur when studying the 'that'. Perhaps it is truer to say that there are certain core questions or core ideas that persist at every stage but which are studied in different ways and in different materials with each age group. Moreover, although understanding of the human situation and of how individuals and groups interpret it in the light of their intuitions of reality is always the aim, we shall be more concerned with the nature of human life in the early stages and more concerned with the intuitions and the values that flow from them in the higher parts of the school. A chart of the subject is shown on page 140.

To describe in detail the content and methods that this type of religious education would require goes beyond the scope of this book, and probably ought to be left to the syllabus makers and the teachers who, knowing the local situation in which the teaching has to be done, would be able to take into account ephemeral and local interests, the materials available and the needs of the classes that are to be taught. The aim here has been to suggest a possible programme for religious education that would have shape and wide justification, based on the assumptions that questioning and rational argument about religion (provided it is backed by accurate and personal knowledge) is of the essence of the subject; that it should help pupils to respect moral and religious values to use religious language accurately and to hold converse about beliefs and commitments; and that it ought thereby contribute to an understanding of the world in which we live.

CORE IDEAS ALWAYS PRESENT	THE CHIEF CONCERN AT EACH STAGE	TYPE OF MATERIAL NEEDED
	FIRST STAGE	**FIRST STAGE**
Who am I? What is the world like? Why is anything here?	Sensitivities and awareness	Stories, poems, music, art, movement
What are other people?	**MIDDLE YEARS**	**MIDDLE YEARS**
How should I treat them? Who will help me decide?	Ideas, questions and language	Facts, symbols, ceremonies, rites, story – its special functions in myth, legend, parable and sacred literatures – and the language of poetry
What is the meaning of life?	**UPPER SCHOOL**	**UPPER SCHOOL**
How can I make sense of experience?	Values and explanations	Codes, customs, ideas and beliefs – the expressions of a people's religious or other philosophical understandings of life

Sundry Difficulties

It is improbable that this restructuring of religious education will solve all the problems or appeal to everyone. Those who see religious education as a more confined and missionary activity and wish it to be conducted with the conviction that one specific way of envisaging reality is true beyond question, will view it highly critically and even with acute distaste. They may wish to ask questions about it which deserve answers.

The first question is whether to conduct the subject in the way suggested is to reduce its influence or to render it antipathetic to religion. What is proposed is not intended to abolish or dilute religious education or to diminish its importance. It is envisaged that religions will be dealt with in schools as carefully as before (if not more so) but that the study of them will win greater educational respect and greater pupil involvement by having added to it certain related studies and by its being set in a context that will allow it to contribute fully to the task of equipping students to understand the diverse world in which they have to live and to deepen their knowledge of themselves and of their beliefs and motivations. One cannot think that it would be more detrimental to religion than the 'perfunctory and uninspired'[12] teaching that has sometimes passed for religious education. It is the duty of the school to educate and the duty of the religious bodies to win converts, but presumably the task of conversion will not be impeded by schools turning out adolescents who have a balanced and informed view of religion and who are able to think about it. If one wants to recruit a bank clerk it is preferable that he should understand the fiscal system and have a sane view of money, rather than that he should be so bored by finance that he shies away at the sight of a pile of banknotes, or is so unthinkingly attracted to them that he compulsively stuffs them into his pockets. Similarly, it is of greater advantage to religious bodies if schools are producing adolescents who have a sane attitude to beliefs and the effects of believing, rather than adolescents who are so bored and scornful that they are blindly and ignorantly switched off to them, or who are equally ignorantly, but bigotedly, switched on.

Another question which religious people will want to ask is, Where does God come in? Should not adequate religious education be based on belief in God? The question arises from the confusion caused by the fact that the term 'religious education' is applied both to the teaching that religious bodies give to their adherents to strengthen them in their faith, and to what is done in schools. The 'religious education' that is provided in church is able to start with the idea of God, taking it as granted and building up on it. But that is too narrow a base for 'religious education', in the other sense, in schools, where a universal belief in God does not pertain. Many pupils in them do not have a belief in God and resent the assumption that they do. To start with a belief in God makes the subject remote and unintelligible to such pupils. Furthermore, in a state school we are not in a faith situation where all are agreed on what the term 'God' denotes. If we are hoping that religious education will assist students to understand the many religious forms they are likely to encounter in a pluralistic world, it will be necessary to introduce them to the idea that the word God may mean different things in different forms of religion and, in addition, that it has no meaning for certain life-stances.

For these reasons the type of religious education being explored and advocated in this chapter does not start from the concept of God as a given point. Nor does it see its purpose as the fortifying of the belief in God, even though it may well have that effect with certain pupils. The concept of God is something to be studied and understood rather than something to be taken for granted.

That does not mean that the idea of God will not frequently enter in to the study. From an early age children hear the word God and want to know what it means. At first their ideas will be crude and mechanistic, and will need deepening and refining if they are not later to class the concept as childish and scorn those who use it as foolish. Later still they may begin to see how the lives of certain folk are significantly changed by belief in God, and be led to investigate what that change is, and the reasons for the belief that causes it. Perhaps they can then appreciate how many use the term God to describe what they find significant in their search for meaning in experience, and in the senior school they might proceed to a philosophical consideration of how far the idea of God provides an adequate, satisfying and structured understanding of experience. All the while they will be learning how men use the word God and are affected by belief in God, and also working out in what sense they themselves can accurately use the word God, what concept they have in mind when they do so, and in what ways that concept is likely to influence their attitudes and decisions. This seems more truly an education in religion than persuading them to a verbal acceptance of a word to which they attach only an imprecise and confused meaning.

At present discussion in a senior school about God tends to split the class into believers, who assert that there is a God and that he is the answer to all problems, and unbelievers, who assert that there is no such thing and that there is nothing more to be said. Neither attitude is an educated one and both are first-rate discussion stoppers. It would be better for religious education to aim to produce pupils who will have been prepared, by their earlier study, to be willing and equipped to undertake a serious and sympathetic, but critical, discussion of the nature and effect of belief in God, and to be able cogently to express their opinions about the concept of God, even though some of them would still find the idea unacceptable. The notion of God is too pervasive of religions not to take up considerable time in religious education, but if the teaching is to justify the term 'education' as well as the term 'religious' it must include an exploration of the meaning of the term and not be based on the tacit assumption that we all know what it means, accept it, understand it, and react to it in an identical fashion.

Finally there is the question of whether the term 'religious education' can properly be applied to the sort of syllabus and teaching that is being contemplated, since it goes beyond a study of traditional religions. Is not a new name needed? This might be no bad thing, both in the interests of accuracy and on other grounds. Teachers sometimes state that one of the greatest obstacles they meet is caused by the word 'religion' in their subject title. It is repelling pupils who have a widespread notion that religion is an unreasonably puritanical fantasy[13] or a fanciful sentimentality, the study of which they contemplate with impatience and disgust. A new name seems desirable though no one has so far had the ingenuity to suggest an appropriate one.[14] A case can be made for retaining the term 'religious education' for an education in values on the grounds that the word 'religion' may be derived from a Latin root meaning to bind and that a man's religion is the vision or set of ideals to which he binds himself and which is therefore ultimately formative of his life style. If we use the word religion in that sense, then we can continue to refer to what has been advocated in this chapter as religious education, since it is intended to help pupils understand the way men make themselves and their life-consistency by their bindings. If the extension of the syllabus in that way is educationally justified, and if it solves some of the problems and opens up new possibilities for the teaching then its name is of minor – even minute – importance. There seems no good reason for refraining from teaching something that is worthwhile because the title is of poor fit.[15]

NOTES

1 Schools Council Occasional Bulletin, *A Groundplan for the Study of Religion* (1977, p. 1).
2 Parliamentary Debates (Hansard) H.L. 383, 68, 701–2.
3 M. Warnock (1979, pp. 33–4).
4 Board of Education, *Educational Reconstruction*, H.M.S.O., 1943, p. 36.
5 Department of Education and Science, *Education in Schools. A consultative document*, H.M.S.O., 1977.

6   Department of Education and Science, *A Framework for the School Curriculum*, H.M.S.O., 1980, para. 28.

7   Department of Education and Science, *The School Curriculum*, H.M.S.O., 1981, para. 27.

8   Quoted in Loukes (1961, p. 98).

9   M. Warnock, *op. cit.*, p. 2.

10   J. P. White (1973, p. 47).

11   J. P. White, *op. cit.*, p. 83.

12   The phrase is used by R. A. Butler to describe religious education in certain schools between the passing of his Education Act and the writing of his memoirs, *The Art of the Possible* (1971), and is found in that book on p. 124.

13   Cf. Reinach's definition of religion as 'a sum of scruples that impede the free use of our faculties'.

14   R. Acland in *We Teach Them Wrong* (1963), suggested the title 'Life Discussion Period', but one hesitates to think that would have made the subject more palatable.

15   Juliet would have agreed. See *Romeo and Juliet*, Act 2, scene 2.

BIBLIOGRAPHY

ACLAND, R. (1963) *We Teach Them Wrong.* London: Gollancz.

ALLPORT, G. W. (1955) *Becoming: Basic considerations for a psychology of personality.* New Haven, Conn.: Yale University Press.

AYER, A. J. (1946) *Language, Truth and Logic.* London: Gollancz.

BARTSCH, H. W. (1953) *Kerygma and Myth.* Translated by R. H. Fuller. London: S.P.C.K.

BOARD OF EDUCATION (1938) *Secondary Education with special reference to Grammar Schools and Technical High Schools* (The Spens Report). London: H.M.S.O.

BOARD OF EDUCATION (1943) *Educational Reconstruction.* London: H.M.S.O.

BRAITHWAITE, R. B. (1955) *An Empiricist's View of Religious Belief.* London: Cambridge University Press.

BRITISH HUMANIST ASSOCIATION (1975) *Objective, Fair and Balanced.* London: British Humanist Association.

BROPHY, B. (1967) *Religious Education in State Schools.* Fabian Society Tract 374. London: The Fabian Society.

BULTMANN, R. (1958) *Jesus Christ and Mythology.* New York: Scribner.

BUTLER, R. A. (1971) *The Art of the Possible.* London: Hamish Hamilton.

CARDUS, N. (1970) *Full Score.* London: Cassell.

CHURCH OF ENGLAND BOARD OF EDUCATION (1970) *The Fourth R* (The Durham Report). London: National Society and S.P.C.K.

COX, E. (1966) *Changing Aims in Religious Education.* London: Routledge and Kegan Paul.

COX, E. (1967) *Sixth Form Religion.* London: S.C.M. Press.

COX, E. (1977) *What it means to be Agnostic.* Ely, Cambs.: Ely Area Resource Organisation (EARO).

DEPARTMENT OF EDUCATION AND SCIENCE (1967) *Children and their Primary Schools* (The Plowden Report). London: H.M.S.O.

DEPARTMENT OF EDUCATION AND SCIENCE (1975) *A Language for Life* (The Bullock Report). London: H.M.S.O.

DEPARTMENT OF EDUCATION AND SCIENCE (1977) *Education in Schools. A consultative document.* London: H.M.S.O.

DEPARTMENT OF EDUCATION AND SCIENCE (1980) *A Framework for the School Curriculum.* London: H.M.S.O.

DEPARTMENT OF EDUCATION AND SCIENCE (1981) *The School Curriculum.* London: H.M.S.O.

DODD, C. H. (1938) *The Authority of the Bible.* London: Nisbet.

DONOVAN, P. (1976) *Religious Language.* London: Sheldon Press.

ELLIS-FERMOR, U. (1941) *Masters of Reality.* London: Methuen.

FLEW, A. and MacINTYRE, A. (eds) (1955) *New Essays in Philosophical Theology.* London: S.C.M. Press.

GOLDMAN, R. J. (1964) *Religious Thinking from Childhood to Adolescence.* London: Routledge and Kegan Paul.

GOLDMAN, R. J. (1965) *Readiness for Religion.* London: Routledge and Kegan Paul.

HARDY, D. N. (1975) 'Teaching religion: a theological critique.' *Learning for Living*, 15, 1, Autumn 1975.

HARE, R. M. (1952) *The Language of Morals.* London: Oxford University Press.

HICK, J. (ed.) (1977) *The Myth of God Incarnate.* London: S.C.M. Press.

HIRST, P. H. (1972) 'Liberal education and the nature of knowledge', in DEARDEN, R. F., HIRST, P. H. and PETERS, R. S. (eds) *Education and the Development of Reason.* London: Routledge and Kegan Paul.

HIRST, P. H. (1974) *Moral Education in a Secular Society.* London: Hodder and Stoughton.

HULL, J. (1974) *School Worship: An Obituary.* London: S.C.M. Press.

HYDE, K. E. (1965) *Religious Learning in Adolescence.* Birmingham: University of Birmingham Institute of Education.

HYDE, K. E. (1975) 'The home, the community and the peer group', in SMART, N. and HORDER, D. (eds) *New Movements in Religious Education.* London: Temple Smith.

INSTITUTE OF CHRISTIAN EDUCATION (1957) *Religious Education in Schools.* London: S.P.C.K.

JOAD, C. E. M. (1942) *Guide to Philosophy.* London: Gollancz.

LEESON, S. (1947) *Christian Education.* London: Longmans Green.

LORD, E. and BAILEY, C. (eds) (1973) *A Reader in Religious and Moral Education.* London: S.C.M. Press.

LOUKES, H. (1961) *Teenage Religion.* London: S.C.M. Press.

LOUKES, H. (1965) *New Ground in Christian Education.* London: S.C.M. Press.

MACY, C. (1969) *Let's Teach Them Right.* London: Pemberton Books.

MINISTRY OF EDUCATION (1963) *Half Our Future* (The Newsom Report). London: H.M.S.O.

NORMAN, E. R. (1977) 'The threat to religion', in COX, C. B. and BOYSON, R. (eds) *Black Paper.* London: Temple Smith.

PAFFARD, M. (1973) *Inglorious Wordsworths: A study of some transcendental experiences in childhood and adolescence.* London: Hodder and Stoughton.

PEATLING, J. H. (1977) 'On beyond Goldman.' *Learning for Living*, 16, 3, Spring 1977.

PETERS, R. S. (1963) 'Reason and habit: the paradox of moral education', in NIBLETT, W. R. (ed.) *Moral Education in a Changing Society.* London: Faber and Faber.

PETERS, R. S. (1966) *Ethics and Education.* London: Allen and Unwin.

PETERS, R. S. (1967) *The Concept of Education.* London: Routledge and Kegan Paul.

BIBLIOGRAPHY 147

PHENIX, P. (1964) *Realms of Meaning: A philosophy of the curriculum for general education*. New York: McGraw Hill.

RAMSEY, I. M. (1957) *Religious Language*. London: S.C.M. Press.

ROBINSON, E. (1977) *The Original Vision: A study of the religious experience of childhood*. Oxford: Religious Experience Research Unit, Manchester College.

ROBINSON, J. A. T. (1963) *Honest to God*. London: S.C.M. Press.

ROBINSON, J. A. T. (1965) *The New Reformation?* London: S.C.M. Press.

ROSEN, H. (1971) 'Towards a language policy across the curriculum', in BARNES, D. (ed.) *Language, the Learner and the School*. Harmondsworth, Middlesex: Penguin Books.

SCHOOLS COUNCIL(1971) *Religious Education in Secondary Schools*. Schools Council Working Paper 36. London: Evans Bros.

SCHOOLS COUNCIL (1977) *A Groundplan for the Study of Religion*. London: Schools Council.

SCHOOLS COUNCIL (1977) *Discovering an Approach*. London: Macmillan Educational.

SMART, N. (1968) *Secular Education and the Logic of Religion*. London: Faber and Faber.

SMART, N. and HORDER, D. (eds) (1975) *New Movements in Religious Education*. London: Temple Smith.

SMART, P. (1973) 'The concept of indoctrination', in LANGFORD, G. and O'CONNOR, D. J. (eds) *New Essays in the Philosophy of Education*. London: Routledge and Kegan Paul.

SMITH, J. W. D. (1969) *Religious Education in a Secular Setting*. London: S.C.M. Press.

SNOOK, I. A. (1972) *Indoctrination and Education*. London: Routledge and Kegan Paul.

STARKINGS, D. (1980) *Some Perspectives of the Settlement of Religious Education in England, 1944*. Unpublished M.A. thesis, University of London.

TAMMINEN, K. (1974) 'Research concerning the development of religious thinking in Finnish students', in *Character Potential: A Record of Research*, 6, 4, February 1974.

TEMPLE, W. (1942) *Christianity and the Social Order*. Harmondsworth, Middlesex: Penguin Books.

TILLICH, P. (1962) *The Shaking of the Foundations*. Harmondsworth, Middlesex: Penguin Books.

UNIVERSITY OF SHEFFIELD (1961) *Religious Education in Secondary Schools*. London: Nelson.

VIDLER, A. R. (ed.) (1962) *Soundings*. London: Cambridge University Press.

WARNOCK, M. (1979) *Education: A Way Ahead*. Oxford: Blackwell.

WHITE, J. P. (1967) 'Indoctrination', in PETERS, R. S. *The Concept of Education*. London: Routledge and Kegan Paul.

WHITE, J. P. (1973) *Towards a Compulsory Curriculum*. London: Routledge and Kegan Paul.

WRIGHT, D. (1976) 'Editorial: Some thoughts on moral education.' *Journal of Moral Education*, 6, 1, October 1976.

Index